SHADES of ME

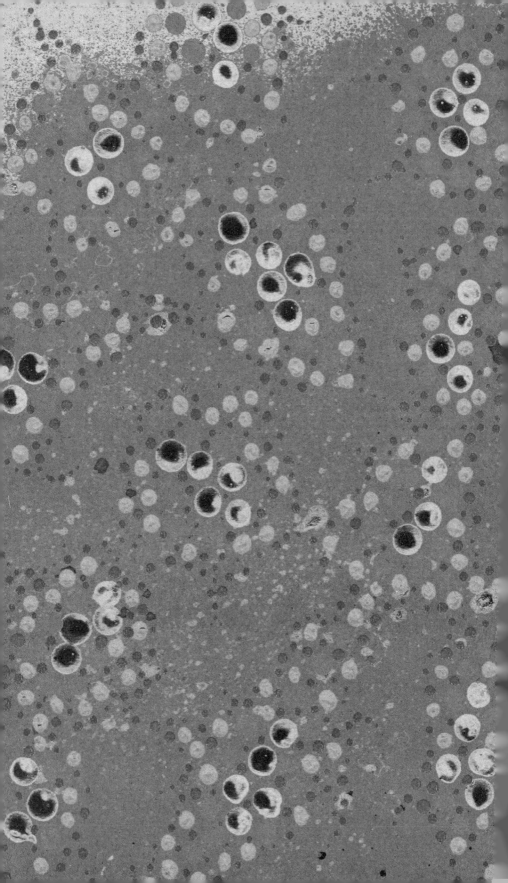

My many lives through many Dreamings

SHADES of ME

Mel Brown

GELDING STREET PRESS

We would like to acknowledge the many Australian
Aboriginal lands that make up our Country.

We wish to humbly pay our respects to the ancestors of the
past and thank them for the courage and resilience they
have passed on to us during their journey on this earth.

We want to respectfully acknowledge the Australian
Elders and Aboriginal peoples of today, as we have the
responsibility to shape our future and role model our
strength and wisdom for our younger generations.

To our future generations who have yet to begin their journey
or even walk on their Country, we eagerly look forward to
the future they will create and the pride they will bring to us.

To our other brothers and sisters with whom we share
our land, we ask for your respect and understanding to
enable us to walk our journey and continue to be the
proud Australian Aboriginal people that we are.

This publication may contain references
to people who have passed away.

A Gelding Street Press book
An Imprint of Rockpool Publishing
PO Box 252, Summer Hill
NSW 2130, Australia

www.geldingstreetpress.com
Follow us! ⊚ geldingstreet_press

Published in 2024 by Rockpool Publishing
ISBN: 9781925946529

Design and typesetting by
Sara Lindberg, Rockpool Publishing
Story and structural editor Gabiann Marin
Edited by Lisa Macken

A catalogue record for this
book is available from the
National Library of Australia

Printed and bound in China
10 9 8 7 6 5 4 3 2 1

*In moving forward, we need
to first look backward to better
understand and prepare
for the journey ahead.*

– UNKNOWN

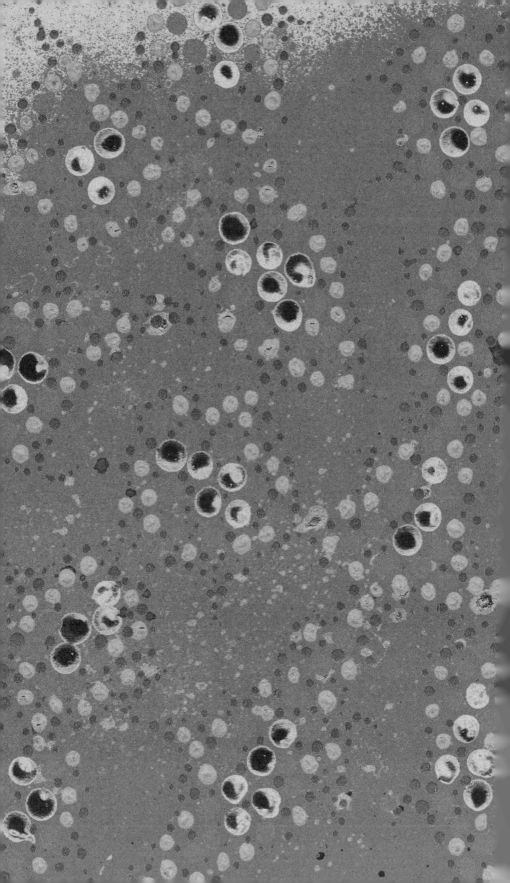

PREFACE

Dadirri is inner, deep listening and quiet, still awareness. Dadirri recognises the deep spring that is inside us . . . It is something like what you call 'contemplation'.

– Miriam-Rose Ungunmerr

Dadirri is a place of inner peace, where time is everything yet waiting for that time to arrive is the true essence of the lesson that is learned. Dadirri is an inner journey of self-reflection, of everything taking place at the right time and in the right order. Wait and listen to Mother Earth: she will lead you on your journey. Dadirri is also the journey of my past that brings me to my present. It is a time for understanding and self-reflection, and what makes me the woman I am. My life is not random; it is deliberate and therefore defined by my journey.

The idea of my Aboriginal ancestors haunted me until I finally acknowledged them as part of my life and brought their meaning into my way of seeing the world. Dadirri, I now understand, is my Dreaming. I see my life as a journey and as a story that is uniquely my own, but in each new chapter my journey allows me the opportunity to experience events and feelings that enrich my life and the lives of those whom I share it with. Every choice I make leads to another seemingly unconnected chapter of my story. Some chapters are filled with fun, laughter and love, and others are sad and filled with anger, hurt and regret. Each one, however, is part of me and weaves to form my unique Dreaming: a story that is still being written and yet to be created.

My Dreaming is the culmination of all the events and experiences that shaped me as a woman, mother and wife. It's about those crossroads in life where the very next step could mean anything from disaster to pure happiness . . . and I've experienced them both and everything in between.

I look forward to the day when there are no more crossroads, the day I can relax in the feeling of having finally fully achieved that elusive inner peace and higher level of understanding. I know that rather than being a destination, inner peace is a journey: a long, vast highway on which I navigate. I will continue driving on that highway with its off-roads and heavy tolls and occasional blissful long stretches where I can hit the throttle and tear down the asphalt, windows down and wind streaming through my hair and just enjoying the ride.

AUTHOR'S NOTE

This story has dark elements, but it is not a story of despair. It is, instead, a story about love, both good and bad, returned and badly used. A story of broken hearts, a story of love lost and found, and my greatest loves of all: my husband, children, family and the love for self that you can find if you are truly, totally honest in who you are.

Trying to find a balance is really challenging for me because I feel a responsibility to ensure I don't traumatise people who are reading my story. I have a duty of care to my readers, which I take as seriously as the duty of care I have for my clients – many of whom have also been through difficult life events. I do not wish to cause further harm or trigger additional trauma, particularly for those who don't have support, yet it is important to tell these stories. Not just the difficult, traumatic elements, but the hope and joy that can be found even in the darkest times by navigating through and out of tunnels of depression, hopelessness and abuse. It is uniquely my story, but it is not a story too dissimilar to the stories of the one in three Australian women who have experienced similar situations of violence, loss and trauma.

I think that is why I have struggled to write this book: because there is darkness here, but also unexpected humour. I don't use humour to undermine the truth or impact of the events themselves but rather to reconcile the past and make sense of what had happened to me. Trust me, there were times that without humour I would not have been able to write about some of the experiences I share in this book. However, humour can be a way to avoid truly experiencing the depth of emotions, and while it is important to have moments of lightness – which exist even in the darkest of times – I also have allowed myself and you, dear reader, to experience some of the hard times I experienced in their full complexity and darkness. I owe it to myself and to you, and to those many other women who have experienced or are still experiencing these situations. Our stories deserve to be told in all their messy, hard, emotional glory. Through doing this I hope I have shown that there is light at the end of the tunnel.

To repeat, this is not a book to retraumatise or trigger anyone, and if you do have difficulty with any of the content presented please use this as an opportunity to seek support. I have provided contact details for some of the services that are available at the end of the book.

Note that some names have been changed to protect the innocent . . . and not so innocent.

INTRODUCTION

It is 1 am. I arrived in England yesterday, and I'm wide awake while the world outside my window sleeps. My mind is plagued with a million thoughts; I'm unsure if it is the effects of jet lag or just the pure excitement of being here. I can't explain why, but being here feels like a homecoming, like being in the embrace of a mother who welcomes me with unconditional love despite the fact I have never before set foot on the shores of England. I cannot explain the connection I have with this land; perhaps it will become clearer as my story unfolds. Now, in this moment, I am sitting on a hotel bed in Scarborough, England beside my beautiful man, trying hard not to disturb his sleep as I feel compelled to begin the first chapters of my story.

I've spent most of my life telling other people's stories – for a court report, an affidavit or a parenting assessment – but in none of those stories was I allowed to include the feelings of those who told them and those whom the stories were about. They were clinical observations, recorded in such a way that facts were the primary and sometimes sole focus of the stories themselves. I had written about other people's trauma for the past 40 years, so I was experienced in providing factual information that could be held up in any court of law in this country. However, telling my own story was different. It was raw and painful and real, and the only way to tell it is to include the messiness of emotions, the complexity of contradictions and the truth that sometimes I didn't act in ways that were obviously rational but were always a true and necessary response to the trauma and events as they occurred.

Here I was, though, in the small hours of the morning in the dark of the English countryside trying to tell the story of a woman who grew up and experienced life in Australia.

I am not English and had never stepped on English soil before this moment in this life, yet there was a connection there for me. My life to that point had been characterised by a discovery of connections, of finding who I was and who I am: not just in this life but in the many lives before it, in my ancestry and spiritual history. A part of my Dreaming has been to recognise that I was not just the woman who sat there that day, but have been many women, men and children going back into the ages as life after life unfurled. This life had been a difficult one in some ways, but also a wondrous experience where I had started to understand the true timeless depth of my Dreaming. It had been a life in which I had been able to embrace the fact that in this incarnation I was many things: Aboriginal, Australian, mother, daughter, woman, wife, writer, spiritualist and ancient spirit. It had not been easy, embracing all of who I was. I'm still learning about parts of myself, thinking about how events in my past – all of my pasts – have shaped me, and how I am also more than any of the things that happened to me.

Our hotel looks out over an ancient castle, no more than ruins really, that sits on an escarpment like a sentry on the hill overlooking the ocean. It is beautiful, but also ravaged by time and the scars of hundreds of years of battles that have left their legacy on this once magnificent artifice. It has all the features that modern-day castle builders would look for, and is in the perfect location to spot and repel approaching enemies or impress visiting friends with the majesty of the great Atlantic Ocean.

Once a long time ago – so long ago in fact you could start this story with 'Once upon a time' – this was someone's home, a place where families were protected from the threats beyond the walls. It was their haven from the outside world, a place to love one another, raise their families and live their own Dreaming.

Earlier that night while walking back from dinner the remains of the castle were surrounded by an eerie glow from the floodlights that lit the remnants of the ancient structure. I thought about how the castle was once regal and formidable but now sat like an elder whose health was beginning to falter and wane but whose memories and stories were as clear as when they were young. Those stories were etched into the stone turrets and written upon the crumbling steps as they patiently waited for a kind ear so they could retell their tales, sharing with others the things that shaped them and made them who they were, the moments that defined them and how they became their Dreaming. As I walked I thought about the stories she could share, this ancient ruin of stone and memory, if she could talk, about what tales she must have of her Dreaming from the many hundreds of years she had sustained life: her triumphs, sadness, battles and joys all that shaped her into the regal old lady she was today.

Now, in these early hours of the morning, I am sitting in a wing chair looking out at that castle on the Hill. The floodlights that lit her so beautifully earlier this evening have been extinguished and she blends into the darkness around her, a dark shadow almost impossible to recognise as a once formidable structure. A quarter moon provides the only illumination, and is diffused by scattered clouds that drift across the darkened skies. Only the entrance of the structure can be clearly seen, shining in the reflected moonlight: an entryway that seemingly leads to nothing but darkness and emptiness beyond.

I don't think I have any specific past-life connection to this castle, but I still feel it calls to me. At the time I couldn't help but reflect that this place, illuminated by the spiritual light of the moon, was a literal symbol of a gateway into the past, a metaphor for my journey to enter the time of the before. She was showing me the way to the ancient and untold stories of her past and present Dreaming so that I could think about my own. I understood this to be a sign of where the ancestors wanted my new journey to start, where my Dreaming could begin to be told, so I start to write.

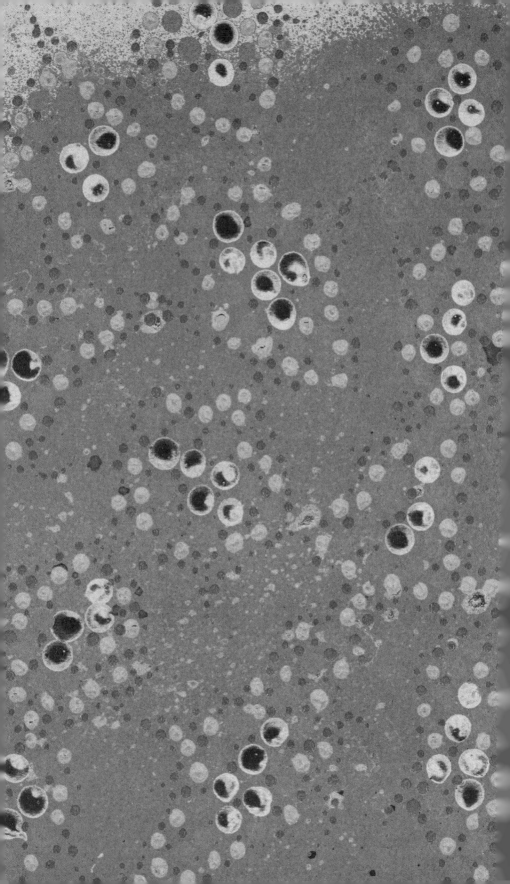

1. BRANCHES

Family is like branches on a tree,
we all grow in different directions,
but our roots remain as one.

– Unknown

To understand my story I start by understanding the stories of my parents and the time and place in which they lived, loved and created me.

My mum fell pregnant when she was 17 years old. It was 1966, a time that seems impossibly different from now and in a place where an unintended pregnancy could spell the ruin of any woman, particularly one so young and of Aboriginal descent. In those days being Aboriginal was something that was often hidden by families and my mother's family were no different, never speaking of their past and surrounding themselves with the camouflage of white Western culture. My mother was raised in a suburban home by a family who hoped to raise their children with good ethics and moral values, and she attended a Catholic school. It was determined at a young age that she would become a nun, a pathway that her surprise pregnancy suggested was never going to be a good fit for her.

My father was an Anglo Australian, and if he knew of my mother's Aboriginal heritage he never spoke of it – at least not when I was a child. She was beautiful, my mother, with alluring eyes and an intelligent bearing, and I think my father fell in love with her with all the fervour and desire that often characterises teenage love affairs. Both were so terribly young, and despite the fact that my mother's parents insisted she and my father get married and legitimise my conception, the two young lovers knew even then that their relationship was probably not strong enough to embrace the birth of a child.

My father's mother Nanna Bess, knowing marriage was not the answer for my parents, offered to raise me as her own, which would allow my parents to have a life without the burdens of parenthood. Nanna Bess told me this story often as I was growing up, and it was always comforting to know that even though my arrival was unplanned and caused a great deal of uncertainty and concern, there was always someone who was willing to love me even before I was born.

I want to be clear here: this isn't the story of a child being born to parents who didn't love them. My parents loved me from the moment I came into this world and have never stopped since, but that doesn't mean they were perfect people or perfect parents, or that they were quick to accept a situation that neither of them had planned or wanted. I can only imagine how Mum and Dad felt at finding out they were going to be parents. At 17 years of age most kids are still at school and enjoying the life that kids are supposed to have. I imagine they considered the overwhelming responsibility of raising a child was more than they could handle.

I think the pregnancy was more difficult for my mum, even beyond the obvious physical impacts. She was raised in a family with strong values who were obsessed with legitimacy and being accepted into the community. No one in Mum's family wanted to stand out, and there was my mother: teenage and pregnant. I have no doubt that her mother was disappointed in her and had no concerns about letting her know. It is a big weight to carry, the expectations of others, and I don't blame my mother for feeling she was unable to do so.

On the other hand Dad, as the second youngest of seven children, had no real expectations placed upon him from his family, who pretty much accepted his somewhat cavalier attitude to life. Finding out he had got his teenage girlfriend pregnant probably didn't fill them with too much pride, but it was a different time then and raising children at such a young age wasn't unheard of. It just wasn't the norm.

So there they were, two young people facing the biggest decision of their lives. Could they really become parents and perhaps never have a chance to live out their own or their families' dreams, or should Mum take the risk to her own life and try to abort this child?

In those days abortion wasn't a legal option and it was rarely mentioned, never mind openly spoken about. There was little opportunity to have the procedure done by a qualified medical practitioner, particularly if you were young and poor, which my parents were. Their only option was to find someone with any kind of medical knowledge who was willing to perform the termination, which was both a dangerous and expensive decision. However, it was their decision to make, and despite Nanna Bess's generous offer they decided to pool their money and seek the services of a disreputable back-alley practitioner to perform a termination

I don't blame them for making this decision; in fact, I totally understand why they did. Life is often full of hard and difficult choices, but in this case as it turned out it wasn't their choice to make. It was mine, and I was determined or, more accurately, *destined* to be born. No matter how hard that abortionist tried to remove me from my mother's womb, I held on.

Mum and Dad realised that, for whatever reason, they were going to become parents, so they got married in my aunt and uncle's backyard. The tenuous union was celebrated by both families but, most importantly, in the pending days of my arrival it made me legitimate, which pacified my mother's already unhappy family. Shortly after the wedding Mum was admitted to Paddington Women's Hospital with complications, where she stayed until I was born a few months later.

I had never asked my parents about my birth story and have no memories of it myself, but years later I did some regression work with a therapist who guided me through that time as though it was all happening right then. It was a very surreal experience but it did feel as though I was being birthed again, which explains why another name for this kind of therapy is 'rebirthing'. During the regression session I remembered a feeling of being in the warm, safe cocoon of the womb then emerging into a world of chaos and being handed to a gentle, kind woman who was not my mother.

When I came out of the therapy session I was doubtful. I knew that when babies were born – even way back then – they were given to their parents immediately after birth, so the memory of this other woman could not be real. I thanked the therapist for the session but left feeling a little disappointed that the regression therapy hadn't worked for me. However, the memory I had experienced felt real in ways I couldn't quite explain, so after a few days of contemplation I called my father's sister, Aunty Maureen, to ask her about the day of my birth.

'Oh, yes,' Aunty Maureen told me, 'your mother had a very hard delivery and experienced some complications right after you were born, so they handed you to me while they attended to her. I was the first one to hold you and I kept you for quite a while till your mum and dad were ready to have you. I was also the one who came up with your name: Melinda.'

This was a light-bulb moment for me. I had always felt a strong maternal connection with Aunty Maureen, and I was beginning to understand why.

Throughout my life I have had a stronger connection with my father's family, particularly his sisters Maureen and Lynda. My connection with my mother's family was less affectionate, and in the earlier years as I grew up I never really felt part of their world. Thinking back now, I believe this was partly due to them seeing me as the reason my mother didn't fulfil her religious future and also, because they were struggling with so many other parts of their lives, they simply didn't have the time or inclination to embrace their first grandchild.

Having begun to understand some of the circumstances of my birth, I was interested to learn more and soon started asking Aunty Maureen all sorts of questions about that time in my parents' lives, finding out so much more than I ever imagined. My mother's decision to have a termination was shocking at first, but as I learned more about her and her way of seeing the world I began to understand that, for Mum, life wasn't quite the same as it was for my dad and his family.

My mother is the second oldest of four kids from Ngunnawal country, in what is now called the Australian Capital Territory (ACT) or Canberra. Growing up I never really understood what this meant, as I had little to do with her family when we were very young because we lived in Sydney for much of that time, while Mum's family remained in the ACT. As an adult I began exploring my birth story and it started me thinking about how life may have been for my mum, who had to think about things differently from how my white aunties had to. Don't get me wrong: life is hard for all women, all mothers, but beyond just the fear of being a new mother and getting through the pain of childbirth, my mum also had additional fears from being an Aboriginal mother giving birth to a child in a white hospital.

I knew enough about our history to understand that back in 1966, when I was born, it was common practice to remove Aboriginal children from their mothers and rehouse them with white families or place them in missions to become servants and workers for white families. The thinking was that Aboriginal families were not as safe, loving or secure as white families and that Aboriginal children would be better off integrating into white society.

It was also a practice to take children from single or poor white mothers, but Aboriginal women were particularly vulnerable. Mum was worried that the nurses would recognise her as being Aboriginal or notice if I came out particularly dark skinned and whisk me away into the night. However, at the hospital, possibly because Mum was a legitimately married woman surrounded by my dad's 'white' family or because my mother's skin was quite light coloured, or perhaps because she and her family had never openly discussed their Aboriginality – even between themselves – or a combination of all of these things, there was no suspicion from any of the staff that an Aboriginal baby had entered the world. Mum later told me about her fears that the hospital would notice my Aboriginal nose but, apparently, I must have slipped their detection or possibly I just had a nose like most babies.

This practice of taking Aboriginal children did not just happen in hospitals, but also in communities. A dark and uncomfortable part of Australian history, it is now known as the Stolen Generations and its effects still play out in many ways for us as Aboriginal people today. The trauma we have passed on through each generation impacts our health and well-being, and ultimately our overall outcomes and experiences of life. Being removed from family, country and culture left invisible scars on many of those who experienced it, and it was no surprise that my mother, as an Aboriginal woman, was terrified of it happening to her and her baby. My mum feared we would become yet another Aboriginal family separated and destroyed by racist and unjust government laws.

Perhaps it was this apprehension that I would somehow be seen as an Aboriginal baby that led to the fact that my Aboriginality was never really mentioned to me as I was growing up, and it meant I never realised I was of Aboriginal descent until I was well into adulthood.

When my sister Shannon was born almost five years after me I think my mother was still a bit fearful but, having already had a child, the hospital staff had little reason to suspect that Shannon was anything other than my mother's second 'white' child – even though Shannon is darker than me and has more of the stereotypical Aboriginal features.

I pretty much ignored Shannon's existence when she first came into the world. The shock of no longer being the only child was mitigated by pretending that she simply wasn't there, and mostly this worked out fine for both of us. Until, that is, the day Shannon, aged around two, decided to pull a pot of boiling water off the stove and spill it all over herself. She was being babysat at the time, and I can only imagine the horror that poor woman must have felt when she saw my baby sister screaming in pain in the kitchen after being doused with searing hot water. It resulted in second-degree burns over many parts of Shannon's body and hands but luckily the water completely missed her face. She had to stay in hospital for what seemed like a terribly long time and it made me realise that I was quite upset that she was hurt. While she was away I even missed her a little bit.

I remember Mum and Aunty Maureen talking about taking goldfish to the hospital in the hope that Shannon would be encouraged to try and catch the fish as a way of keeping her fingers from fusing together. I'm unsure if this was just a seven-year-old's interpretation of an overhead conversation or whether it actually occurred, and I'm very hopeful this technique was not used, but I never could get that image out of my mind. By this strange means my little sister became real to me in ways she had never really been before. Thankfully Shannon fully recovered and her scars mostly faded over time. She has no memory of the scalding or her time in hospital.

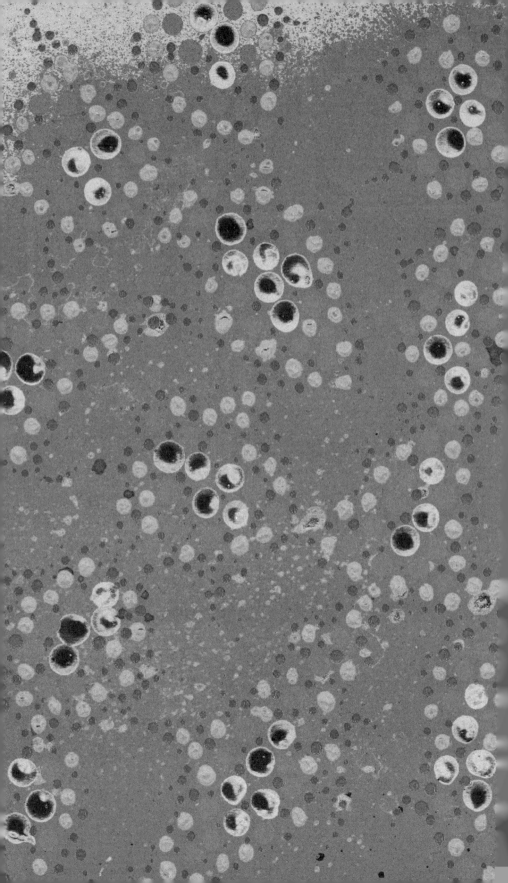

2. FRACTURES

I have accepted fear as a part of my life, specifically the fear of change . . . I have gone ahead despite the pounding of the heart that says: turn back, turn back.

— Erica Jong

Throughout my childhood Shannon and I were often with babysitters, because both my parents worked to keep a roof over our heads. Dad bought his first concrete truck when he was in his 20s, and he and my mother worked hard to try and build us a proper home life to raise me and my sister.

Our first real family home was in a new suburban development west of Sydney called Blackett, in the Mount Druitt area. Back then – it was 1971 – it was like a wild frontier and not too many people were brave enough to conquer the outer Western Suburbs of Sydney, but the opportunity to realise the Australian dream of owning a house was too much for my parents to resist.

Living out west was okay but it took me away from my dad's family in Mascot, which was almost an hour's drive away. I missed them greatly, and looked forward to the times we travelled there to visit. I particularly missed my dad's mum, Nanna Bess, and my cousins, as I had spent most of my earlier years growing up alongside them.

I learned over the years that even tightknit families can fracture and relationship ties begin to fray through misunderstandings, the pressures of distance and diverging life paths. That has certainly been the case with me, as events, burdens and strains on my parents caused a number of family rifts to appear. However, my dad's youngest sister,

13

Lynda, who is about 15 years older than me, has always been my constant, the one member of my family who I knew would stick by me through thick and thin. No matter what stupid decisions I made or successes I had, Aunty Lynda was there sticking by me. She was the first person I would phone when times were tough or when times were wonderful, and mostly for no reason at all. Later, when Lynda had her own daughter, Tia, I became more of an aunt than a cousin. It's still the same: nothing has changed but the crappy grey hair that seems to have taken over both of us.

It wasn't all bad in Mount Druitt. Mum bought us a fluffy Samoyed dog we called Snowball and built a pool out the back, which was a great respite in the searing heat of a western Sydney summer. We were happy enough, and my mum did her best to raise us while working and looking after our home. She was obsessed with cleanliness: everything had to be bright, shiny surfaces and no mess could be visible. I can honestly say I have failed to live up to my mother's expectations of spotlessness, although I do keep things relatively clean. I am amazed at how immaculate she kept our house considering how busy she was with everything else on her plate. Looking back, I think she had a belief that her house had to be cleaner than anyone else's because there was so much negative stereotyping about Aboriginal women being dirty or unkempt, and she needed to prove them all wrong. At the time, though, it was annoying that I was constantly berated if I left a bowl on the countertop or tracked mud in from the backyard.

Dad was far more laid-back: nothing ever seemed to worry him, and he glided through life on a cloud of chilled-out obliviousness. He wasn't really suited to the role of father/family man. In his way, I think he tried his best to be a good husband and father but he was so easily distracted – and there were many distractions for my dad, such as other women, alcohol, motorbikes and FJ Holdens. I guess he just wanted to act like an ordinary bloke of his age, hanging out with mates, going to the pub and living a free and easy life, so I don't think he really settled down till he was much older.

Women, particularly, proved to be his downfall. Quite often when Mum left Dad to look after Shannon and I we would find ourselves dragged off to odd houses where Dad would disappear for a few hours with strange, nice-smelling women, leaving us to play in the house sometimes with a random kid who also lived there. Dad never told us to keep these visits a secret but, somehow, we instinctually knew not to talk about them. In fact, as we grew older he often openly talked about his conquests as a younger man, but I think under the bravado there was some shame. I know this because he's a good and generous man who hates to hurt others. Maybe it's just the dad that I know today is different from the young man from 50 years ago.

Later, when I reflected as an adult on my issues with boyfriends, I often thought about how my father's behaviour helped shape my responses when the men in my life cheated on, disrespected and betrayed me but, even then, I couldn't judge Dad too harshly because I know both he and my mother were forced by circumstances – namely the circumstance of me – to enter into a marriage neither of them really wanted. It's not surprising, then, that my parents' marriage didn't last long beyond my seventh birthday.

Mum and Dad were together for such a short time and have been separated for 50 years, so the concept of Mum and Dad as a single unified entity isn't really something I have much experience with. Even writing 'Mum and Dad' in the same sentence feels strange, as though they don't really belong anywhere together: even in a story.

I don't remember too much about their separation. What I do remember is Mum packing us into the back of her FJ Holden, with a mattress resting precariously on top of our belongings on the back seat. The mattress served as a bed so Shannon and I could sleep during what was then a long trip from Sydney to Canberra, which was where we were headed – though no one explained this to me at the time. Two small children unrestrained on a mattress in the back seat may sound extraordinary to us now, but back then seatbelts were optional extras and kids quite happily held on for dear life in the backs of cars, utes and even motorcycles.

The trip to Canberra was long and uncomfortable as Shannon and I bounced around on a mattress that until a few hours previously had belonged on my bed. We were on the road for more than five hours in an unreliable car on poorly maintained roads, often driving through dense fog and miserable grey rain. It turned out to be a good introduction to my new life in Canberra, which was to be much less cheerful than my previous life in Sydney: a life that was growing further away with every mile we travelled.

During that car ride was the first time I remember feeling true fear, the kind that creeps into your body and settles there; a stubborn resident in your very bones. I'm sure I had felt fear before; I was a fairly normal kid and would have been scared of many things, but this was something different. Mum and Dad had mostly hidden their marital problems, the fights and tearful accusations that accompany any breakdown of trust and disintegration of a marriage. Neither Shannon nor I had any understanding of why we had suddenly been piled into a car and whisked away from our home, school and friends or, more importantly, why our dad wasn't coming too.

This was the start of my experience of feeling terribly, totally alone even if other people were around, because everything could change without reason or explanation and my whole world could suddenly be taken away, as I was taken from my home and father. He might not have been a good husband, but he was a great dad and I loved him so much.

As we headed off down the Hume Highway I didn't know that, for Mum, this was her journey back to her family, a family we kids hardly knew and had seldom spent time with. If I had been given the choice I would have made it clear I wanted to stay in Sydney with Mum and Dad and my dad's family – aunts, uncles and cousins I had grown up with – but no choice was offered, and the car headed relentlessly inland towards a future I had no control over and to a family who were strangers to me.

3. LOST AND ALONE

*Loneliness is not just about being
alone, but feeling alone even
when you're with someone.*

– UNKNOWN

My fears were not totally unjustified, as even after we moved in I never truly felt like part of this new maternal family or that my grandparents particularly liked me. Maybe they knew I didn't want to be there so they decided they had better uses of their time than to spend it with an ungrateful child who didn't appreciate being in their home.

I know if I ever openly voiced this with my mum's family, even now, they would deny it, defiantly attesting that my maternal grandparents loved me just as they loved all their grandchildren and treated me no better and no worse. I think they would even believe this to be true, but kids are aware of deeper truths. Children haven't developed the skills to understand and justify adult behaviour and see things for what they are: unadulterated pure truth. I never felt as though the relationship was as warm as with my paternal grandparents – and to a young child, my grandfather was a little scary.

I spent much of these early years in my grandparents' house as a solitary child who just sat or hid in the lounge room behind the lounge, trying hard not to be noticed. From the age of seven onwards I learned how to put on the mask of the quiet, obedient child, regardless of how miserable or terrified I was really feeling. My mother's family would describe me as being polite and somewhat shy, and probably assumed my happiness hovered below the surface of my timid demeanour. I even remember being given a T-shirt as a young girl that featured one of the seven dwarfs on it. Under the print of the shy little dwarf, who awkwardly looks up with an apprehensive expression, was the name 'Bashful', but I wasn't bashful: I was lost, and trying really hard not to be taken away again. No wonder everyone always said I was such a compliant child. I think I was shit scared most of the time.

In all fairness, my grandparents did the best they could to provide us with basic care. Love, though, seemed an added extra they simply weren't able to provide, even to my mother, never mind to my sister and me. As I grew older and found myself working in the community and welfare sector I was able to better understand that my maternal grandparents each had their own stories and experiences that shaped them into the individuals they were, and it was these experiences that prevented them from giving me the love that was so freely bestowed upon me by my paternal grandparents. Luckily for me I had unconditional love from Nanna Bess.

Nanna Bess was a tiny woman – so small she had to buy her clothing in children's sizes – but as small as she was I doubt anyone was ever born with a bigger heart or capacity to love without judgement. She used to whisper to me, 'Nans aren't supposed to have favourites, but you're one of mine.' Maybe this bond was established during those very first days of conception when she wanted to raise me, when she loved me before she even knew me and wanted to make me hers.

Unfortunately, trips to see Nanna Bess were as infrequent as those to see my father, and it often felt as though I was living a million miles away from my Sydney family. Yet even at a distance and despite the breakdown of my parent's marriage, my dad's family made sure they let us know they cared about us. They always made sure Mum and us kids were included in family events, they never missed a birthday or Christmas card and frequently called just to let us know they were thinking of us and wanting to know that we were okay. We spent as many school holidays as possible travelling up to Sydney to spend time with my paternal aunts, uncles and cousins, escaping what had become my life without them in it.

Mum did her best as a single mum, trying to make sure we attended good Catholic schools and had all the things other children and families had even though I never understood how she ever managed to afford it. She was determined to give us a life as close as possible to the middle-class one we had started out with as a family in Sydney, but the simple fact was that circumstances were different now and our lives were different too. Mum was very young, barely 25 and trying to make her way in a world that was not kind to women, particularly working single mothers.

I don't believe I could have done as good a job as Mum if I had been in her place. She was alone, living with two daughters who were too busy trying to make sense of why their whole world had been upended to ever think about making it easier on her. Her strength and resilience are truly astounding to me now, although regretfully unappreciated by the small child I was back then. She never gave up, never gave in. Once my mum makes her mind up to do something there is no stopping her from getting it done, and luckily for us she made her mind up to give us the best life she could and she did everything to try to fulfil that promise.

Not all of our Canberra family were as bad as I might make it sound. In fact, over time I developed great and strong bonds with several aunties, uncles and cousins. I had a particularly strong bond with my mother's brother, Uncle Bernie. Uncle Bernie is my godfather, and he takes that job seriously. I don't remember him before moving to Canberra, but he often told me I did know him when I was very small, before Shannon was born, because he lived in Sydney then and loved caring for me and hanging out with me all day while my parents worked.

When we moved to Canberra we lived for a while with Uncle Bernie and his wife, Aunty Coral. I loved my uncle, but I didn't like living with them! Aunty Coral made us eat weird food, strange, foreign stuff like tomato pasta and foul-tasting curries. I was used to the bland Australian diet of meat and two veg, so these odd concoctions filled me with dread. I would scrunch up my nose, but I knew the rules were always to eat everything on your plate or you would have to go to bed hungry. I remember eating tiny morsels and preferring the feeling of a rumbling tummy than the lingering taste of those hateful flavours on my tongue.

Dad was also still in the picture, if far away. We went up to see him every second weekend, often flying Ansett as unaccompanied minors.

I loved those weekends, being with Dad and visiting Nanna Bess, Aunty Maureen and Aunty Marie – the undisputed matriarchs of the Sydney clan. While I was in Sydney I felt like I used to feel: a member of an ordinary middle-class, well-off, well-educated white family and with people who openly loved and cared for us.

As young as I was I understood these people were my real family, and I wanted to be just like them when I grew up: strong and loving and always able to solve any problem that came along. When Mum and Dad split up I felt lost and alone, and even though I had my sister I never felt as though I belonged anywhere. I couldn't understand why Mum had taken us there and perhaps formed a rather unrealistic view of my dad in the process. Dad was still his unsettled self, going through women without any thought for the future. I had little understanding of this as a child but there are some memories of him that, thinking back, indicate that Mum's decision to make Canberra our permanent home was probably the right one.

4. SAYING GOODBYE

How lucky I am to have something that makes saying goodbye so hard.

– A.A. MILNE

In my young mind my dad moved through women with regularity. Mostly these women are blurry, half-remembered images of blonde or brunette hair and the smell of perfume or cigarette smoke, but occasionally one has stuck in my memory – often for the very worst reasons.

This was the case with a girlfriend my dad introduced us to when I was around eight years of age. She was a nice enough woman but a little vague, with three children of her own and one just a baby no more than five or six months old. On this particular visit to Sydney, Shannon and I arrived just a few days after the baby had been released from hospital after a severe case of whooping cough.

I was playing with Shannon and the woman's other kids in the bedroom when I heard the baby crying, and I saw my dad's girlfriend go over to check on her infant. For some reason I had a bad feeling, so I followed the woman to see what she was doing. She started changing the child's nappy and I could hear that the baby was breathing strangely. The woman didn't seem to notice; she just carried on changing the nappy as though nothing was wrong, even as the child started coughing and gasping for air.

Once she realised something was awry, Dad's girlfriend didn't seem to know what to do. She just stood there like some kind of zombie, waiting for the coughing fit to pass. After a moment the baby did stop coughing but, unfortunately, the baby had also stopped breathing. The woman seemed unfazed, not panicked at all, as she casually picked up the now-silent baby and walked out the back door and into the yard, where she began to unceremoniously drop the baby's tiny, quiet body into the garbage bin.

As I watched this unfold in front of me it took a moment to realise what had happened, but then I was screaming and calling for Dad, who rushed outside and quickly grabbed the baby on its way into the bin. He somehow managed to get the child breathing again, wrapped the baby up and took it inside. The whole time the girlfriend just stood there disconnected, like she was watching a particularly boring movie that someone else had picked for her and not the rescue of her own child.

I don't know what Dad said to her after that, but the next time we visited Dad that girlfriend and her children were gone, disappeared from Dad's life as though they had never been there at all. I could almost convince myself the incident never occurred, that I had imagined the whole thing except that Dad remembered it too.

I wish I had been older then, had known more, because that woman was clearly experiencing some kind of trauma. Her behaviour wasn't normal, but it is something that I later encountered versions of many times while working with traumatised and mentally ill women. I can only hope she found the help and support both she and her children desperately needed, although I suspect she didn't. Services for women are inadequate now, back then I doubt they even existed at all.

However, I was a child and my years working with traumatised women were a long way in my future. At the time I don't believe I gave her a second thought because I was coping with my own worries and concerns. It seemed that life was always about saying goodbye to Mum or to Dad. Every visit to Dad was shrouded in dread, because no matter how much fun it was it always ended with tearful goodbyes and a trip back to our 'real life' in Canberra. Maybe we weren't the first kids to have divorced parents, but it sure felt that way. I never did meet any others who had their hearts broken every second weekend like we did. Perhaps those other kids did exist, but if so they were as good as I was at hiding the sadness lest anyone see the hurt and brokenness inside. Even now I hate saying goodbye and will do anything I can to avoid it. Truly, I would rather just walk away from people saying nothing than to say goodbye. Even the word is irritating: 'Good bye.' Ha! There is nothing good about it.

I guess that's also the invisible effect these constant partings had for me. I never was able to work out that in some situations 'Goodbye' is the very best thing you can say to someone, particularly if it means you never have to see them again.

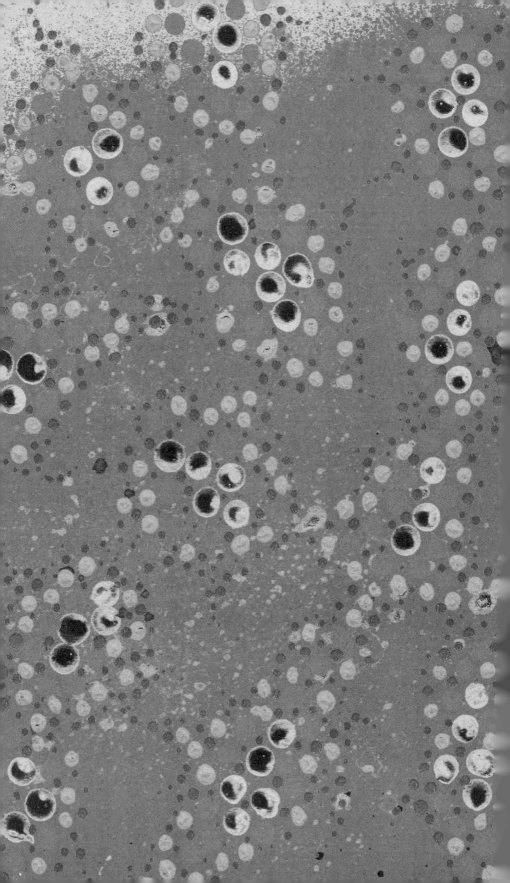

5. FAMILY IS FAMILY

Family is family. Whether it is the one you start out with, the one you end up with, or the family you gain along the way.

– GLORIA, *MODERN FAMILY*

In 1976 when I was 10, out of the blue Dad decided to move his concrete truck to Goulburn, driving each day between there and Canberra. I was overjoyed to have Dad back but sad that our fortnightly visits to Sydney were now at an end, and I would have to wait until special family occasions to see my Sydney aunties and Nanna Bess.

I guess it was inevitable that once Dad was in Canberra, he and Mum would get back together again. Unfortunately, it was equally inevitable that it was not going to last. Within a short time of him moving back a woman started visiting the house when Mum wasn't home. It was déjà vu, as she brought along her kids and the group of us played in the yard or, if it was too hot or rainy, watched TV while this woman and my dad disappeared for hours at a time into the bedroom.

Of course, Mum found out. Maybe Dad told her or maybe she discovered it some other way, as the woman, Jackie, was a friend of them both as they all belonged to the same tenpin bowling league. Jackie was often there with her two girls, who I have to say I didn't like that much. To be fair, I didn't really like Jackie either; she barely had two words to say to Shannon and me. The oldest was shy and had red hair, and the younger one had attitude and sass that really should have belonged to the redhead. I had little choice but to put up with them all, though, as this woman enjoyed her clandestine visits with my father.

I hoped Jackie and her kids would be gone for good once Mum found out about her, but instead Mum unceremoniously threw Dad out. He quickly, and I suppose unsurprisingly, announced he was moving in with Jackie and her children. It was just a matter of time before she became his new wife and that object of all young girls' secret fears: the dreaded stepmother.

Mum also moved on . . . well, moved backwards, some might say. She met an old friend, someone we had known when we were living in Mount Druitt, a fella named Roger who had been the father of my best friend Rosie in infant school. We had lost touch with them when we moved to Canberra, or so I thought, but then suddenly he was there now single and separated from his kids, who were living with their mother in Wagga Wagga.

I didn't mind at first. Roger was familiar and funny and often delightfully unpredictable, announcing we were going out for ice cream in the middle of the night or a road trip to the beach on a hot afternoon or giving us presents. I was only nine years old then and didn't realise that 'spontaneous' and 'fun' were often synonyms for 'drunk' and 'irresponsible'.

After we had been living with Roger for some time he brought his children home to live with us. Last I knew they had been happily living with their mum in Wagga, and now in the middle of the night they were being slid into sleeping bags on the floor of my bedroom. Shannon and I woke up the next morning with three new sisters! Apparently, Roger had driven to Wagga, beaten up his wife's boyfriend and taken the girls.

Our life changed quickly from that point. My old best friend Rosie was now my new step-sister and, abracadabra, two sisters became five overnight. I have sometimes wondered how that fitted into my mum's plans, her responsibilities increasing almost instantly from being a mother of two to a mother of five girls. Think about that: five girls with seven years difference from the eldest to the youngest, but she never complained and me, Shannon and my three new step-sisters all thought it was great fun.

To add complications to an already complicated situation my dad and Roger, my new unofficial stepdad, had been good mates in Sydney, knocking around together, drinking and hanging out. Pretty soon Dad was coming over with Jackie and our families naturally blended together. I couldn't have been happier: it was like I had all the benefits of my mum and dad when they were together without any of the tension. We somehow all managed to get on, and this unconventional extended family was surprisingly successful in all of the ways that mattered. Roger also seemed to be fitting in well, his spontaneity being a great source of joy for me and my sisters.

One particular day us five girls decided to ride the bus to meet with Roger at the department store where he worked. As we got on the bus we didn't see that our new little kitten had escaped the house and followed us down to the bus stop. We only realised she was there as the bus was pulling away and we saw the tiny little kitten running across the main road, only to be hit almost instantly by a car. Trapped in the bus, there was nothing we could do to help her and all five of us burst into hysterical tears and cried all the way into Woden.

What a sight we must have been to Roger as we came into his store, a crowd of little girls stained with tears and barely managing to get the whole story out between bouts of hysterical sobbing and wailing. Roger, however, was quick to act. He gathered us all up, got us into his car and spent five hours driving up to Sydney to buy us a new pet! Cuddling our fluffy new puppy on the trip back, I am ashamed to say every single one of us girls had pretty much forgotten about our dear departed little kitty cat.

Another time we were on holidays down the south coast at Batemans Bay. Mum as usual had to work and couldn't come. One night, after dinner we were hustled into the car for a quick trip home to visit Mum but, unbeknown to us, she had jumped in the car with the same intent. We passed each other in the middle of the night and we had to drive back down the coast the next morning to find Mum waiting for us.

This may sound a bit frenetic, but it was one of the few times in my young life when I didn't feel alone and helpless. With the five of us girls and the life we lived there wasn't time to be lonely. Our house was filled with crazy unpredictability, and I loved every second of it.

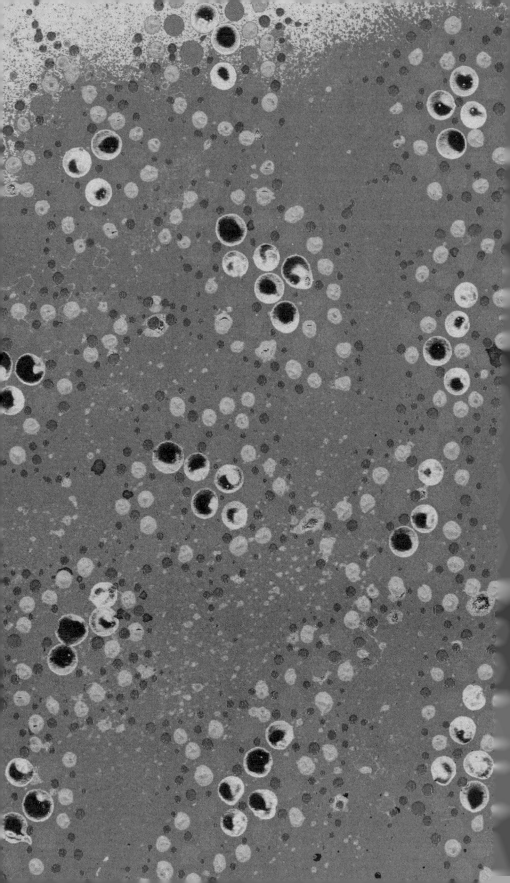

6. BURDEN

Family isn't always blood, it's the people in your life who want you in theirs: the ones who accept you for who you are, the ones who would do anything to see you smile and who love you no matter what.

– MAYA ANGELOU

By the time I was 11 years old Dad had settled in Canberra with Jackie and her two children. These girls – Elena, aged seven, and Hannah, five – were a lot younger than me and I often ended up being an unofficial babysitter for them as well as to Shannon, as Dad and Jackie disappeared for an evening out or a quick drink at the pub. I didn't dislike the girls as much as I had when they were really little, but we still weren't true friends. On the cusp of my teenage years, I was too busy growing up and trying to sort out my own life to worry about how these little girls, who had also been thrown into a totally new family, were feeling.

It didn't help that Jackie and her family did as little as they could to make me and Shannon feel part of their extended clan. We didn't see Jackie's family often, as her mother and father lived on a property somewhere in the middle of rural New South Wales at a place I believe is called Middle of Nowhere, just 10 miles up from the town of It's Too Hot for Anyone to Want to Live Here.

In the summer of my eleventh year me and Shannon, along with our two paternal step-sisters, found ourselves travelling with Dad and Jackie towards an isolated spot, passing nothing but endless seas of wheat fields broken up by patches of scrubby bushland and the occasional weathered old homestead in the distance. Dad and Jackie were planning on attending the yearly car club show, but this year they weren't taking us and we would instead be staying with our new step-grandparents for a week.

We drove up to the house and got out, happy to stretch our legs after hours of hot, cramped driving. Back then air-conditioning for an FJ Holden was called 'WD40': windows down at 40 miles per hour. There were no seatbelts and no radio, just four little girls sitting snugly in the back of the car with sweaty legs touching each other and fighting with each other for sitting too close.

An old woman came out of the house and greeted us. This, it turned out, was our new step-grandmother. She gathered our step-sisters in her arms and smothered them with hugs and kisses, but she paid me and Shannon little mind. This seemed weird to me, because Elena and Hannah had met my family in Sydney many times and they always greeted them with open arms, almost as long-lost family.

This was a place, it was now apparent, at which we were expected to stay until Dad and Jackie returned from the car show.

I was never a bedwetter but I became one during this week. I shamefully tried to hide my wet sheets under the guise of offering to wash the sheets on all of our beds. I'll credit my step-grandmother: I think she knew what I had done but never embarrassed or scolded me, but it did little to strengthen our bonding experience.

Aside from the step-grandparents' disinterest, I quite liked being on the property. We spent much of our daylight hours on the farm tramping around the bushland and uncleared areas, trying to find some shade from the unforgiving sunlight and avoid the sheep that listlessly stood around the arid paddocks. The area was in drought, as much of Australia's rural properties so often are. Sheared to almost comical baldness, the sheep did what they could to find any grass or weed left for them after the ghostly grey kangaroos, which seemed in number far more numerous than the small flocks of sheep, had chewed them almost to the ground.

As we tramped together through the bush, keeping a close eye out for snakes that wanted to kill us and huge kangaroos that gave us the stink eye while sizing us up for a fight, and wandered up old, rutted dirt roads we started to grow closer and even become friends, in a way. Even so, I was as happy as a kid on Christmas Day when Dad and Jackie returned and bundled us all into the car. There wasn't a single complaint about the sweaty legs resting against mine as the wind blew through the windows and we headed out on the four-hour journey back to Canberra.

When I look back at myself, a child roaming the bush with my sister and two step-sisters – all four of us in nature in quiet contemplation, feet in the dirt, listening to the whispers of the shrubs and silence of the nearly-empty dam, where the yabbies struggled to maintain life as the water around them dried up – I realise that this was when I felt my heart truly open to the first stage of my Dreaming and I began the journey of Dadirri and an understanding of the true meaning of family.

I hadn't learned it all yet, but it was a good beginning.

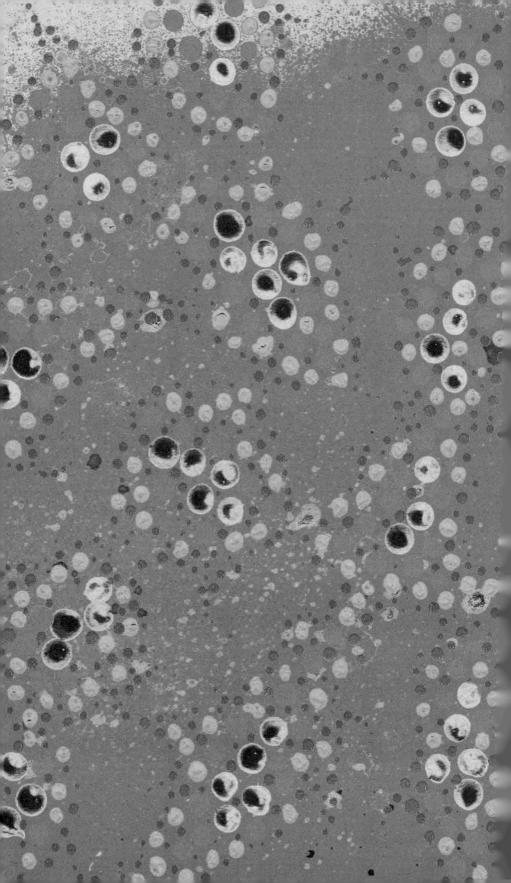

7. ROGER

The shattering of a heart when being
broken is the loudest quiet ever.

– Carroll Bryant

Things in my new family were going as well as could be expected.
I was seeing my dad regularly during our weekend visits and had
settled into our somewhat unsettled routine. If this was life then
I could handle it, even if I did wish I could live with Dad full time.
Then my step-sisters decided to ruin it. I don't suppose they meant to,
but they did just the same.

We were travelling back to Mum's house at the end of one of our
weekend visits with Dad. For some reason Elena, Hannah and Jackie
had decided to tag along this time, so we four girls took our snug
seats squashed into the back seat of the car. At least being the eldest
meant I always got a window seat, so I could crack the window down
and look out and ignore the others wriggling around on the seat
beside me.

I wasn't even listening to the conversation that was going on, as
Shannon, my step-sisters and Jackie were playing some lame driving
game. Then my ears pricked up: Elena had said something I couldn't
believe. In the middle of the game she had referred to my dad as 'Dad'.

Her dad!

He wasn't her dad; he was mine. Mine and Shannon's, but to my
11-year-old way of thinking he was mostly mine. You see, I had always
been Dad's girl ever since I had been born. Shannon was Mum's and
I was Dad's: that was just how it was, so who in the hell were either
of my step-sisters to claim him as *their* dad? Didn't they have their
own father somewhere? And who said I was up for sharing mine?
I certainly hadn't given permission for sharing, and I wasn't going to.

33

These little girls who had pushed their way into my family and into my heart, whose mother had stolen my father away from us, now thought they could claim him too! I hoped I had misheard but, no, there they were saying it again, the pair of them. Surely Dad would say something, would remind them that he wasn't actually their dad at all, but he didn't say anything. He just continued driving, returning us to our other family.

I have no idea what else those girls said in the back seat of the car that day. I don't remember anything but that single word, seemingly repeated over and over again. Dad. Dad. Dad. It was like a drill in my brain, and the world stopped for me at that moment. I was shattered: hadn't I lost enough? Hadn't these girls taken enough from me, living with my dad while I only got to see him on weekends? It was so unfair, and now they were claiming him as their own.

There was nothing I could do, nothing I could say, so I sat there waiting for that endless drive to finally be over, to arrive at Mum's house so I could jump out of that car and away from those horrible little criminals who were stealing my father. I couldn't tell you how long that ride continued. All I know is that I spent the rest of it staring out the window, willing myself not to burst into tears.

I did not forgive my step-sisters for that, not for years. I don't know if they understood that they had broken my heart that day. I wasn't an aggressive child and I didn't act out or anything; I just refused to engage with them. We became strangers and remained that way until much, much later, when I was a teenager. Later as an adult I had the maturity and insight to see that those little girls were as lost and unsettled as I was and as much in need of a dad. At least mine was there for me. Their dad had left them, never even caring enough to keep in touch. I understood then what I couldn't as a child, that they were as stuck as I was and just trying to make their best way through it. At the time, though: oh, how I hated them.

Despite that I look back at those years of my late childhood as some of the happiest. Our families were somewhat settled and we were all managing to get along. Mum and Dad were friends and I got to spend time with both of them, and I didn't even mind living in a house with Roger or sharing a room with Rosie. Maybe this is the reason why I don't tend to dwell on or even really remember the violence and threat that was present even then, lurking at the edges of my memories daring me to confront it, then and later in my life. I realise I lived in denial of this violence and the effects it would have on me for a very long time.

Roger's drinking started to become even more pronounced, and sometimes when he got a particular dark look in his eye, a particular squint, a particular set to his jaw or furrow in his brow, he would change from the fun-loving man we adored into someone hard, violent and frightening. More than once the mean version of Roger turned on us without warning. Quick as lightning, his arm would shoot out to capture whichever child was unfortunate enough to be within grabbing distance, and then lift her off the ground and slam her into a wall.

These were silent and terrifying attacks that came without warning and ended almost as quickly and unexpectedly as they had begun. Roger didn't discriminate: Shannon, me or one of his three daughters were equally likely to be targeted when his temper rose and his need to lash out became overwhelming.

I vividly recall one moment when I was standing innocently in the kitchen and I must have done something to set Roger off, because suddenly I was dangling in mid-air, my face level with his, pinned between his fist and the wall, his spittle flying in my face as he yelled about some perceived slight, some tiny misdemeanour I had no idea I had been guilty of.

It didn't happen every day, but it occurred often enough that the anticipation of it happening kept us all on eggshells, quick to take Roger seriously if he raised his voice or warned us to stop doing something we were doing. I used to think that Roger himself was never sure when he might turn nasty, when his lovable side would disappear and be replaced by this suburban Mr Hyde. I even believed he felt truly remorseful when his bad behaviour was spent and he was faced with frightened, tearful children, but that wasn't true. Roger knew exactly what he was doing when he targeted one of us, because years later I realised he never lost his temper or lashed out in violence when Mum was around, and I never thought to tell her what he was like when she wasn't there.

Like most children who are the victims of violence I felt it was my fault, that if I was better behaved or less troublesome Roger wouldn't get mad. I also wanted to keep our family together because I had already experienced a broken home and had no interest in being part of another. So, I stayed quiet. Perhaps that was why we all did.

At the time I was sharing a room with Rosie, and we were often awoken by Roger as he stumbled into our room in the dead of night, usually drunk, and demanded our attention. 'How much do you love me, girls?' he would ask. Rosie was more experienced at this than I as she had grown up with this behaviour, and from copying her I knew the only answer that would not attract his sudden and frightening wrath was to loudly and confidently say, 'Up to the moon and back again.' He would sigh happily if we said this and lie down on one of our beds, often but not always falling into a drunken sleep for a few hours. The phrase 'Up to the moon and back again' still makes my blood turn cold.

It's funny how even at an early age we may not be able to find the right words for what we are feeling, but instinct takes over and we somehow know when things are not right. During those drunken late-night visits, Roger made me feel . . . not right. He never touched me or Shannon during the night-time visits, but a few years later Mum came home early from work and found him in bed with Rosie. Part of me wishes I had spoken about him back then, had told Mum or even Dad about what was happening even if I didn't know the full extent of it, but as I already mentioned I was a quiet and shy child and I wanted to keep our family together, even if sometimes that family felt a bit frightening.

As it turned out, Roger and his night-time visits to his daughters was not the thing that destroyed our family, although he was at the very heart of the implosion that occurred.

8. IMPLOSION

Not every story has a happy ending, but
it doesn't mean it's not worth telling.

– LUCIAN

The end of our family as we knew it began the year I turned 12 years old. I don't remember the exact date, but I do know it was the week my beloved Nanna Bess visited us from Sydney. I had been looking forward to seeing her and was eager for Dad to come and pick us up for our fortnightly weekend with him, knowing that Nanna Bess would also be there.

I was packing clothes in my room when the yelling started, so I can't say with any certainty what may have set it off. Mum and Dad had gone through two separations and Dad's infidelities together, yet I couldn't recall a single time I had ever heard a raised voice between them. Suddenly here they were, my mum screaming blue murder at my father. The sound sent chills down my spine and I had that odd feeling again, the kind I had experienced a few times before that something really, really bad was happening.

Still I hesitated, not sure what the right thing to do was. It was only when I crept down the hallway towards the increasing commotion that I saw Shannon and my other sisters sitting huddled on a bed together. The fear in their eyes was a reflection of my own, but I told them to stay in the room and closed the door, then hesitantly walked down the hallway towards the kitchen, where the yelling was coming from.

The first thing I saw as I came down the hallway was Mum standing in the kitchen with a knife in her hand, waving it at my dad. Dad was standing facing her. Both of them were angry and yelling at each other, and I remember screaming at Dad to get out of the house because I was scared something might happen to him. Dad turned to me, and his hand fell from his chest and revealed a bloody stain on the front of his shirt. I cried out as I realised that Mum still held the knife and was continuing to advance on him. She had stabbed him. She had stabbed my father, right there in our kitchen.

Hearing me cry out, Mum turned towards me, her eyes wild. It was the most frightening thing I have ever seen, both before and since. She screamed at me to get back into my room and I obediently complied. Rosie was sitting on the bed, her eyes wide and terrified. Without even acknowledging her I opened our bedroom window and clambered outside, knowing that if I returned down the hallway she would see me, and I ran back into the house through the open back door.

Dad was still in the kitchen, one hand over his bloody chest and the other up in a placating manner towards my mother, who was standing in the kitchen doorway brandishing the knife. She still looked angry, but the wildness had left her expression and she seemed anxious as well as furious. I screamed for Dad to get out, but he just turned to me with a weirdly calm expression and gave me an odd smile.

'Get Shannon and get into the car,' he said. 'I am not leaving you here.'

That set Mum off again, the wildness returning as she stood without yielding. 'You're not taking them. You're not taking them from me, you bastard!' she screamed.

I thought Mum was going to stab him again and I looked around for something, anything, that might stop her. It was then I saw Nanna Bess sitting, shocked and pale, in one of the dining room chairs, watching the scene unfold in a kind of silent horror. I hadn't known Dad had brought her with him to pick us up as a surprise, and there she sat as unable to comprehend the situation as I was.

Mum turned to my father who, after a moment's hesitation, stepped back away from Mum and towards Nanna Bess, taking her by the hand and leading her silently out of the house. I stayed inside, not wanting to make Mum angrier. I watched them drive away, not knowing how this event would change my life in the days, weeks, months and years to come.

I turned back to Mum, but all the fight had gone out of her. She looked like a deflated balloon, leaning against the doorframe of the kitchen for support. 'Go to your bedroom,' was all she could say.

I hesitated for a moment, then I saw Shannon walking up the hallway and hurried down, ushering her and my step-sisters into my bedroom. Rosie was still sitting on the bed and we all clambered up beside her, clutching at each other, none of us sure what had happened or what it meant.

A few minutes after Dad left I heard Mum leave the house and drive away. Roger was not home so the five of us girls were now alone in the house, waiting for some adult to come and explain what was happening or tell us that everything was going to be okay. No adults came and we sat there for what seemed like hours. My head was filled with questions. Was my dad okay? Would he die? Would Mum go to prison? Who would look after us if both our parents were gone? These were all questions that should never run through the mind of a 12-year-old girl, but part of me knew that whatever happened I had just witnessed my family disintegrate in front of my eyes.

The event that changed my life forever happened in the space of five minutes, although it took me several years to understand what had set it off. It was not until I was an adult that I learned Mum's side of it, that she had attacked my dad not because of him – at least, not exactly – but because of Roger.

Roger had begun to pose a real and undeniable threat to my family life. Just a few minutes before my father had unwittingly walked through our front door, Mum had discovered that Roger was having an affair with a woman he had met at work. It was the ultimate betrayal. Yet again my hard-working, faithful, tolerant mother had been cheated on by a man whom she thought she could trust. She had allowed this man into her home and taken in his daughters and cared for them like her own, and she had trusted her already bruised and battered heart to him, but he had betrayed her.

In this heightened state she had opened the door to my father, who walked in as though everything was fine. He might have made a few wisecracks or simply acted in a way that my mother couldn't bear, but I suspect he just reminded her of the history of betrayal she had endured at his hands as well as Roger's and it was just too much. It was the last straw for my mother who had, I now realised, suffered all the slights of her life in silence. Unable to take out all her built-up frustration and rage on Roger, who was luckily for him nowhere to be found, Mum took it out on the other man who had broken her heart.

Mum later told me she didn't really remember how it started, what Dad had said to set her off, and I believe her. I think he probably didn't say anything; his presence may have simply been enough. Perhaps in that moment as my dad and nan walked through the door oblivious of the emotional turmoil bubbling within my mum, all the pain, humiliation, disappointment and heartbreak that Mum had ever known walked right in with them and forced her to feel just how badly her heart was broken.

I am not excusing Mum's actions. At the time I was truly terrified by them and uncertain about how they would affect the rest of my life, but I have learned from experience since then that unresolved feelings and unvoiced hurts have a way of coming back and biting us. While we may think it will make us feel better, unrestrained anger just causes us to act out in harmful ways and make poor decisions that do little to ease our pain, and we often pass that feeling on to others. That is certainly what happened in this case, and Mum came to rue the events of that day far more intensely than any of us realised.

My dad believed the whole thing was simply bad luck on his part, that if he had showed up on another day at another time the whole incident would never have occurred. 'Just bad timing, Grub,' he said.

Maybe he's right, but I'm not so sure. It seems to me that my mum had a lot of unresolved trauma and anger towards him, and eventually it was going to find its way out.

As for my nan, I never found a way to talk about what had happened and we had an unspoken agreement not to talk about it again. That was Nanna Bess's way: always unwilling to focus on the negative or speak ill of anyone. Bad things and unpleasantness were to be safely swept away, not discussed. In Nanna Bess's world love and kindness were the only things that mattered, no matter who you were or what you did.

I think she froze there in the dining room that day, having flashbacks to a time many years ago when in a jealous rage a man had shot dead another man out the front of her house as he believed the man he shot had been showing affection to his wife, who was my nan's daughter. Now she had watched silently as her son had been stabbed by his ex-wife. I think she didn't know how to see it, never mind react to it, so she simply didn't.

I don't know what happened next between Mum and Roger, but they must have come to some resolution because he came back that night and things quickly returned to normal again.

After Dad had left the house that night he drove straight to the hospital, where he discovered the wound was far deeper than he had imagined. The blade had pierced right inside his ribcage, missing both his heart and lung by mere millimetres. Despite this he decided not to press charges, and I think we all hoped that would be the end of the matter.

It wasn't.

Not too long after the incident Mum agreed to let us go back and see our dad. Nanna Bess had left for Sydney by then, so we didn't get to spend any time with her. I was particularly sad about that, but it was the beginning of the school holidays and that meant more time with Dad, which I was happy about.

On the last day of the holidays Dad and Jackie took us aside and asked if we wanted to return to Mum's. Dad was still worried about Mum, about whether living with her was the best thing for Shannon and me. All I was thinking was that I didn't want to return to the house if Roger was going to be in it. I didn't want to be thrown against walls anymore or woken in the middle of the night by a scary drunk who insisted I tell him I loved him to the moon and back again.

Dad's house was quiet. That was what I wanted and that was all I thought about, so I said I didn't want to go back to Mum's and that I wanted to live with him for good. I never thought about Mum or how she might feel about us not coming home. I had no knowledge of her fear that her children would be taken away from her in the hospital by white people after she had given birth, and how Dad and his new white wife taking permanent custody of us might look to her to be a variation of the very same thing. I was just an exhausted and frightened kid trying to make an adult decision in an adult situation I simply didn't have the experience or greater knowledge to navigate.

Because I was the oldest and seemed so set in my decision Shannon didn't even get a vote, and Dad immediately went out and got legal advice to work out how he could keep us with him. His well-educated, well-meaning but ultimately arse of a solicitor advised that it was up to me to go to my mum and tell her to her face that we wanted to live with our dad.

I was 12 years old and scared out of my wits, and I was forced to stand at my mum's front door surrounded by Dad and two police officers and tell her that Shannon and I didn't want to live with her anymore. I don't remember Mum's face as I stood there frozen in place, feeling so awful I wanted the earth to swallow me whole. I don't remember what I said or how she responded as I broke the news that must have shattered her already badly bruised and abused heart.

I loved my mum; she was a good mum. She was hard at times, she was strict, but she worked her arse off to ensure we had more than we ever needed and I had just ripped her heart from her chest and stomped on it in front of my dad and two policemen. I wish I could have told her that I didn't want to leave her, that it wasn't her I was afraid of, that it was Roger and his drunken behaviour, but I was a kid and I didn't have the words to tell her this or explain what I was thinking. All Mum heard from me was that I was rejecting her, that her children no longer loved her and preferred to stay with the man who had cheated on and abandoned her. She was just 30 years of age.

When I look back I am ashamed of this more than anything else in my life. As an adult and mother I can't think of anything that could destroy me more than having my own child not want to be with me. This is what I did to my mum, and I robbed my sister of her mother as well. I will never know or understand how my mum continued to function from that point on or how she ever forgave me, because I am not sure I have ever forgiven myself.

I blame a system that didn't care about the trauma this would cause to a child and a family. It was and still is a system that is only concerned about what they can put into an affidavit to help them build a case.

9. CUSTODY WARS

Breathe. You're going to be okay . . .
you've been in this place before. You've
been this uncomfortable and anxious
and scared, and you've survived. Breathe
and know that you can survive this too.

– DANIELL KOEPKE

Once my statement had been made the lawyers took over. All visits to Mum were negotiated through solicitors, and what followed was a custody battle so bitter that any dignity, compassion or cooperation my parents may have been able to find for each other before was totally stripped from our lives. Secrets they had kept for each other for many years became public knowledge. Affairs, fights, mental health episodes or anything they could think of was aired in open court as each used whatever ammunition they could find to blame and accuse each other of neglect, abuse or carelessness to prove that they, not the other, was the better parent.

The relationship with my maternal grandmother, always frosty, turned downright hostile and she openly declared that Shannon and I were to be removed from her will – in essence, removed from her family – because we had turned against our mother and preferred to live with our dad. I think she was furious that all the dirty laundry about my mother's pregnancy and other issues about our family were being brought up during the custody hearing. She may have felt like this was a reasonable response to the situation we found ourselves in, but I never really forgave her for it. I was a child, and no matter how she may have perceived things I was not responsible for the actions of the adults in my life. I was a bystander to these events as much as anyone.

During this time I had little contact with my mother's family aside from Aunty Joan, who was the lone voice standing up for us chastising my grandmother for being so petty and nasty to us. Her protests fell on deaf ears, and Shannon and I were left without anything from my grandmother except resentment and dislike.

My mum continued to live with Roger and his girls as she fought hard throughout the months the custody case dragged on. It's normally the mother who is victorious in a custody case, where a general consensus is usually that children are better off with their mothers, assuming there is no evidence that the mother is unstable or a danger to them. Mum tried everything she could think of to win but, of course, Dad had the aces up his sleeve: the incident in the kitchen during which Nanna Bess and I had witnessed my mother stab him, and my voice in an affidavit devoid of emotion or rationale declaring I wanted to live with Dad. No matter what the solicitors argued or how much evidence Mum had of my dad's neglect and infidelity, she was never going to win the case. Eventually Dad was granted custody and we were to stay with him and Jackie full time.

It may have seemed like this was what I wanted. After all, I had said as much to my father when he had asked me outright, but it wasn't at all what I wanted. I loved my mother and didn't want to lose her. We did still see her, as the custody arrangement determined that Shannon and I would have weekend visits with Mum a couple of times each month. I loved these times and tried to let Mum know I loved her. Amazingly, she never acted like she was angry with me or blamed me for the outcome of the custody battle, although I knew she was bitter and hurt. How could she not be?

That says a lot about how generous she was and how much she loved us both unconditionally, no matter what poor decisions she may have made beyond that. You see, my mum had not given up despite the court decision. Losing her children was something she just couldn't reconcile with, despite the brave face she presented to us during our custody visits. Although she never directly said anything to us, I knew she was still upset about what had transpired because

I overheard snippets of whispered conversations between her and my aunts, when she spoke about how angry she felt.

On one of our visits I overhead Mum saying she had a gun and was going to 'get them'. I was immediately concerned: who was the 'them' she was referring to? Did she mean my dad and stepmother or was she talking about all of us, including Shannon and me, who had so badly betrayed and abandoned her?

I didn't know whether I should I tell my dad or just shut up and pretend I hadn't heard Mum say what she'd said. I was by then just 13 years old and didn't have the mental ability to process what I had heard, but I felt sick and frightened the whole weekend we spent with Mum and wondered if I *had* heard her say those things or just imagined it. It would be easier to think I had made a mistake than to face the reality of what this might mean, but I knew I really had heard it and was unable to sleep from worrying about what my mother may have been capable of.

The moment I got back home to Dad's I told both him and Jackie what I had overheard. I don't know why I told them, except that I was scared and wanted it to stop being my problem to solve. I wanted the adults to look out for me and themselves for a change and not be forced to solely carry all the hurt of my broken family on my shoulders. However, the moment I told them the house filled with police officers demanding that I retell them exactly what I had heard. I found myself repeating the same story over and over until they were satisfied they had every single detail I could give them. I wasn't sure what they would do because I was just a kid and didn't know how much of what I said would matter. As it turned out, it mattered very much indeed.

The next morning Jackie took off with Elena and Hannah, leaving Dad, Shannon and me to sort the mess out on our own. Shannon and I went to school, but that afternoon my dad got a call from the police telling him he had to take my mother's threat seriously. By that afternoon Shannon and I were on a plane to Sydney, flying to my dad's family, where it was decided we would be safer.

I was glad Shannon and I were safe but I kept thinking the whole time that Dad was still at home by himself. Alone and unprotected, what if something happened: how would anyone know? The week passed slowly, with my sister and I ensconced safely in Sydney. Later that week the police found Mum, and they told Dad she no longer had a gun and that he and the rest of us were safe.

I never quite believed that Mum's threat had been completely empty. There was something about the way she had said she was going to 'get them' that spoke of the determination I knew she possessed. I had a feeling about it, and even back then my special feelings were rarely wrong. However, the police assured us there was no gun and that Mum was not going to come and get us in the middle of the night.

It wasn't until years later I realised the police had said she 'no longer had a gun', which meant that she had at least at some time possessed one. I didn't talk about this with her till many years later, never speaking about it until I was a wife and mother myself. When I did bring it up she openly revealed how close Dad had been to being shot and her imprisoned on a murder or attempted murder charge.

'I really was going to kill him,' she told me when we were seated around the kitchen table, where all the best conversations happen. Then Mum revealed the whole strange and surreal story. Not only had she every intention of killing my father, she took herself off to apply for a gun licence, and then appeared in a gun shop in Queanbeyan to buy her first gun. She told the shop owner she needed the gun to kill kangaroos, which were quite commonly found around the area.

The gun-shop owner took her at her word and tried to sell her a huge-calibre rifle that would 'make mincemeat of those pesky Skippys'. He must have been very surprised when she opted instead for a more manageable gun much more suitable for shooting a pesky ex-husband than it was for the huge grey marsupials that bounded around the suburbs. The fact that the gun-shop owner didn't think this strange amazes me even today.

He sold Mum the gun and she left the shop satisfied that her plan was coming together nicely, despite the fact she had absolutely no idea how to load or shoot as she had never even held a gun before this. However, my mum was a practical woman so she rocked up to her neighbour's house with her new purchase to ask for his help in teaching her how to shoot. He had less idea than Mum about how to use a gun, so it became a farcical case of the blind leading the blind.

Anyone else would have given up at this point, but not my mum. She was nothing if not determined, and she decided the neighbour could do some research then teach her. I'm still unsure if he knew he was part of a more elaborate plan or if he thought Mum really was just taking up a new hobby culling roos in suburbia.

Luckily for my dad the neighbour was struggling financially, and as he was not the brightest bulb on the Christmas tree he decided to burn down his house for an insurance payout. Mum's gun was inside the house and was burned down to ashes. No gun, no murder, so crisis averted. Dad lived and Mum didn't end up spending the rest of her life in jail over a poorly thought-out murder plot!

Of course, as a child I had no knowledge of any of that, just a general uneasy feeling that something terrible was happening. I wasn't able to trust that there was no longer any credible threat till a few months later when Mum left Canberra to move to Moree with Roger and his kids. Shannon and I were unable to see her for regular visits, which I was partly glad about because I wanted to avoid Roger and because I was a little afraid of my mother now, but I was also sad because I missed her terribly.

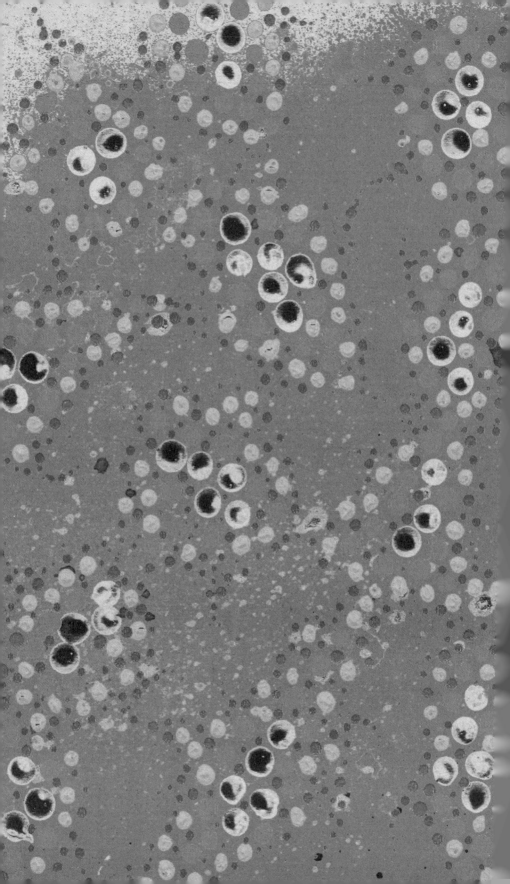

10. THE MOLE PATROL

Normal is an illusion. What is normal
for the spider is chaos for the fly.

– Morticia Addams

Once it became known that Mum was no longer any real threat to Dad, life at Dad's went back to normal. Jackie and her kids, along with Shannon and me, went home to Dad's. Dad and Jackie went back to work and continued their social life and we went back to school. No one ever spoke about it or how it may have affected us. It was as though in their minds it never happened, but it had affected me.

For years after whenever us kids were home alone, which was often, I crawled beneath each window facing the street and closed the curtains so that no one could see us inside. I was worried that Mum still had her plan to get us and was hiding out there somewhere, waiting for a silhouette to pass the window to give her the perfect target for that shot she had wanted to make for many years. As an adult I know how silly this was, but as kids we see the world in black and white, good and bad. It was the way a child makes sense of things that are way beyond their level of comprehension.

Through all of this Mum was still in my life, and later as times grew tougher she never judged me or let me know I had disappointed her in any way. As I grew I began to develop an understanding of what she was going through. I know she would never have hurt myself or Shannon and it was Dad she was angry at, and he was the only one she was intending to target. I still think her decision to try to assassinate my father was reckless, crazy and horrifying but, after my own life experiences of being abused, betrayed and made to feel crazy, I wonder if I would have reacted in a similar way if someone had tried to take my children and painted me as a terrible parent.

The unfairness of it must have been hard to reconcile with, seeing as it had been Mum who had always been the one who had looked after us and fed, clothed and nurtured us. It was she who fought so hard to protect us both, raising us almost single-handedly, and yet there she was, just another Aboriginal woman losing her children to a white middle-class system with no understanding of why it was happening to her. If only we had been able to talk more, to share what was happening to us and been open, perhaps all of the craziness could have been avoided.

I think my mum was doing her best to manage a situation she was unable to control. Hindsight is a privilege when we have time and wisdom at our disposal. Many a bad decision has been made in the heat of the moment and I am guilty of more than a few – maybe not to the extent of the decision my mum made, but I do live my life with some regrets.

Living at Dad's meant changing schools, which I faced with a gnawing dread. What if I didn't make any friends; what if I didn't fit in? I was used to an all-girls Catholic school, and this new high school was going to be full of both boys and girls. I was not sure how I was going to cope.

In my first weeks at the new high school there was another new girl, Michelle, who was tall with long blonde hair and tanned skin just like a Norwegian goddess, and we immediately struck up a friendship. Perhaps I clung to her like she was a lifeboat, terrified I would drown if I didn't make friends with her immediately.

I also soon met Debbie, who was incredibly likeable and had a good nature and ability to fit in with everyone. As Debbie was already part of the cool group Michelle and I were quickly admitted by way of default, although I imagine they weren't quite so happy to welcome me as they were to have Debbie as part of their gang.

This group of girls were the popular mean girls, the kind who always have the right clothes and hairstyles and are lusted over by the boys and hated by the other girls. At school, the nickname for us was the 'Mole Patrol', not the most flattering of terms but it summed up how many of the girls in the group, including me at times, acted towards the other students. The Mole Patrol was tightknit and very

50

rarely allowed anyone else to enter the clique, so I guess Michelle and I were fortunate to be allowed entry at all. It was fun most of the time: we shopped together, did our makeup and hair and talked about boys. Most of the girls in the gang smoked, and we all drank when given the opportunity.

I don't think I realised how mean and arrogant we actually were during our school days, but many former school mates would remark at school reunions about how they were pleased that the Mole Patrol had surprisingly grown into quite nice women. Many others refused to attend the reunions simply because we were going to be there, which I knew because I was involved in organising the school reunions.

Looking back, I can't really blame them: not only were we often nasty, but a lot of girls in our school were envious of us. However, life in this circle of friends wasn't always easy. Female friendship circles and any other groups of people, really, have a kind of default hierarchy that sets in and determines how each member will be treated. There's the leader, social organiser, outrageous rebel and, often, the scapegoat. I got to be the scapegoat for the Mole Patrol, and as a result I felt as though I was barely tolerated and often found myself only just hanging on to my 'prestigious' position. Generally, I felt quite insecure among them. I spent most of my high school years wondering what I was going to face when I arrived at school and encountered my 'friends'. Sometimes I was ignored and at other times I was gossiped about, and one time I nearly got into a fight with another person in our group except that a teacher stepped in and made us sort things out.

Despite this I stayed in the Mole Patrol for three years, partly because it was safer to be part of the group than not be part of the group and partly because, well, there was no way for me to truly understand or deal with the situation I was in.

Later in life I learned about lateral violence and realised that was exactly what I had been experiencing. 'Lateral violence' is the term used for bullying, backstabbing, gossiping and bitching plus a load of other behaviours that happen among a group of peers or people who share a similar oppressed social status, class or situation. They turn on members within their own community rather than on the community that oppressed them. It is similar to hierarchical violence, which is usually orchestrated by higher-status groups on lower-status ones. Many people either ignore or don't take lateral violence seriously, but it is a major issue and particularly for young people, and it can sometimes be so toxic it causes low self-esteem, self-harm and even suicide. This is what some of the girls in the Mole Patrol were doing to me and what I think a lot of young women experience with their so-called 'friends', and it creates toxic and seemingly inescapable relationships within peer groups.

While many people experience lateral violence, working out how to deal with this behaviour isn't easy. It takes courage and confidence to stand up to those in your social circle, family or relationships, and some people choose to live with this behaviour rather than deal with it. It's similar to living with domestic and family violence: the bad is tolerated because you know that essentially your partner is a good person or, at the very least, they may be better than the next person waiting around the corner and certainly better than nobody. That is how I felt about the Mole Patrol.

My experiences with these girls added and contributed in many ways to my own acceptance of violent and disrespectful behaviour. I grew to believe this was the natural way of things, that I deserved it, and that made it very hard to fight back or get away from violent and bullying situations in all areas of my life.

11. JACKIE

In this house the only thing normal is the setting on the tumble dryer.

– Unknown

Life at my dad's wasn't full of rainbows and unicorns but it had some sense of stability and moments of peace, unlike the unpredictability and uncertainty we had lived through with Roger at my mum's house. I lived with Dad and my stepmum for four years, till I turned 17, but it was Jackie who probably featured more during this time. I don't think Jackie really knew what to do with me. Part of her wanted to protect me and embrace me as a daughter to make sure I was well taken care of and happy, but there was another, competing part of her that resented the intrusion that me and my sister's arrival brought to her life.

She had stated on several occasions that inheriting two daughters on a full-time basis had inconvenienced her, sometimes reminding me that her marriage vows to my father had never included an agreement to take on his children. I know now, after having had children and new relationships of my own, how important it is to try to get it right because those children, regardless of their age, are the ones whose lives are really turned upside down.

I also look back on my own mother and realise how quickly and effortlessly she accepted Roger's children as her own, treating those girls exactly as she had her own daughters. Mum never complained about the extra work that unexpected children bring or the way they crowded the already small house, or the fact that they had arrived without notice or consultation. How generous had my mother been all those years, and I had never noticed it. I'd never thought about the strain it must have put on her and her relationship with Roger, and added to her already tiresome labour to keep us all well looked after.

For the most part my stepmother didn't openly complain that taking us on was a burden, but I spent the first year at Dad's in a constant undeclared war with her complete with unexpected and equally undeclared ceasefires. I was grounded a lot during that period.

After a particularly rocky time, I found myself confiding in the school counsellor, who listened sympathetically and arranged for Jackie to come down to the school to have a chat about how I was feeling. My stepmother may not have listened to me but she did listen to the counsellor and things got a bit better between us.

The other big part of my life was the FX-FJ Holden car club, which was Dad and Jackie's main passion. I couldn't drum up too much love for the old classic Holden cars, because for me they were just another car. There were plenty of them in the garage and weekends were filled with even more of them as we gathered with other car-club members. FX and FJ Holdens are a uniquely Australian identity that melds into all my memories of growing up. It was a smooth, beautiful constant in what was often a tumultuous childhood. Mum loved them too and was actually the one who started the Canberra FX-FJ club we were members of, so it was also a connection with her even though she had moved away.

The club provided most of our social events. However, these social gatherings were often fuelled by alcohol, and the aftermath of many a meeting or road trip was an angry argument between Dad and my stepmother. Unlike the hidden animosity between my mum and dad, fights between Jackie and my father were never disguised.

I recall one night while my friend Debbie was staying over Dad and Jackie came home from a car club event yelling their heads off. I was embarrassed that Debbie was witnessing our dysfunctional family in action, so I decided to see if I could intervene in some way or at least make them quieten down a bit.

When Jackie realised I was there she quickly turned towards me, telling me to go back to my room. I did as I was asked, deciding it was better to leave Dad to deal with it.

I returned to my room where Debbie, Shannon and my step-siblings were all gathered. We huddled together, listening to the shouting from the kitchen. After a short time a quiet fell over the house, but all we could do was wait. Finally my dad appeared and hastily collected Shannon, Debbie and me and drove a few streets away to Debbie's house, where her very perplexed parents were woken unexpectedly in the wee hours of the morning to find their daughter dropped at their doorstep. Dad, Shannon and I continued on to the home of one of Dad's mates, where we stayed the night. We returned the next morning, though, and no one mentioned a thing, like nothing had even happened. My dad, and our family in general, were nothing if not expert at the art of avoidance and basic denial.

I didn't understand at the time how my dad could make women so angry with him. To me, my dad seemed like the type of person people couldn't help but love. He always had a joke to tell and was always the first to volunteer to help a mate who found themselves in trouble. He wanted nothing more than to please others and always seemed to find himself in relationships with strong-minded, dominant women who made most of the decisions. He just blended into the background, hoping not to be noticed as he lived his life.

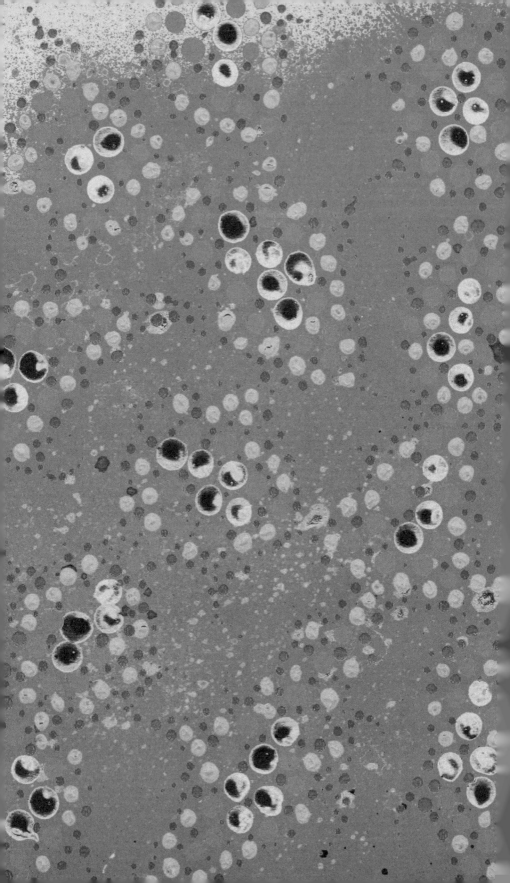

12. LEAVING HOME

Sometimes things fall apart
so other doors can open.

– UNKNOWN

I think the level of trauma I had already experienced in my life increased my tolerance to what bad behaviour was, and I didn't have the knowledge or understanding to expect to be treated with respect and consideration within a relationship as I started my own dating life. After all, it was just the norm for people to cheat and lie and let you down, and for you to love them anyway.

That was certainly my first introduction to love. Not that it started off that way, but then those kinds of relationships rarely do. When I met John he was exciting and attentive, and I thought he really loved me. Weren't love and obsession virtually the same thing? To my 16-year-old mind they certainly seemed to be, and I had little beyond my own experience to go on.

John was several years older, which was of course another completely unseen red flag. He already had a full-time job and a car, and I felt so grown up riding along next to him. Suddenly I was playing with the adults, and as a result I pretended I was more mature than I was as we hung out with his older friends. An age difference of a few years isn't a big deal when you're in your 20s or 30s, but when you're still in school and your boyfriend and his mates are all working, drinking and making their own decisions that age difference becomes a huge divide.

I was never a big drinker. Sure, I had the occasional drink with my friends, but it was mostly just school kids sharing some stolen alcohol someone had nicked from their parents. I couldn't buy alcohol from the local shops because I worked there and they all knew exactly how old I was. They also knew many of my friends, so as a group our access to any kind of booze was pretty limited. However, alcohol was something John had no problem indulging in or getting access to, and he enjoyed drinking.

I should have seen the signs then but I was young, and I had nothing to compare it with and no responsible adults looking out for me. Eventually, after I had been seeing John for a few months, Jackie pulled me aside for a little talk. I fully expected her to warn me away from John, as she knew about his drinking, but she didn't. Instead, she simply told me that a boy of John's age would have certain expectations, and if I was not prepared to fulfil them it was likely he would find some other girl who would. By then I needed little convincing, and if the moment arrived I would need to make sure I had contraception. I really did want to be with John in all ways, so I followed along as my stepmum took me to the local doctor and by the end of that I was on the pill, no questions asked.

I felt as though I was a proper woman and Jackie even seemed to be willing to treat me like one, telling me that as long as I waited the 30 days needed for the contraception to take effect I didn't have to abide by her curfew and could come and go from the house as I pleased. Suddenly, from having so many rules and limitations on my time I was free to stay out as long as I wanted. Perhaps she could see a time when I would no longer be her responsibility, or perhaps she was simply more comfortable with our newly adopted adult relationship.

I should have known better though, because a month later when I finally did stay out into the wee hours with John my furious stepmum called me to her room as I walked in and grounded me on the spot. It seemed that she really didn't think I was an adult, after all. I thought I was, though, and I was desperate to start living a more adult life.

In Canberra high school finishes once you graduate Year 10, and you move into college to complete years 11 and 12. As I reached this milestone I found myself thinking more and more about leaving school and getting some independence. I hated not having any autonomy over my life and saw the prospect of having a full-time job and financial stability as one way I could have a bit more control over what happened to me. I found school boring and longed for the independence I saw in my older friends, who had their own flats and proper full-time jobs, but I had no idea how to go about moving into a more adult life, which I think was why fate once again intervened.

College was a very different experience to high school because you were given a lot of leeway and parents were not contacted if you routinely didn't turn up to classes, the way they were in high school, so my attendance started to fall off pretty quickly. I had a new boyfriend and a heavy work schedule, so it was good to sometimes take a school day off to go and hang out at Pine Island and work on my suntan. I do admit I had more than a few odd days off; in fact, I barely attended college at all.

Perhaps recognising that my absenteeism was not going to get any better, the principal of my school finally organised for me to get an interview at the Reserve Bank of Australia. I easily aced the interview and got the job. Suddenly I was no longer a high school student: I was a proper working woman in a professional job!

Life was good. I had a real grown-up job and a real grown-up boyfriend, and I was making good money working full time at the bank during the week and picking up weekend shifts at my old job at the supermarket. It seemed as though things were finally going my way . . . until my stepmum decided it was time for me to leave home.

This was a complete shock to me, as I had done nothing that I felt warranted this over-reaction. I might have had my issues with my stepmother, but I was always respectful and mostly followed the rules at home. I let her know where I was and I still asked permission to go out or stay over with John, even though I was a full-time worker and earning my own money. I was also paying board and learning the responsibility of contributing to where you live.

However, for some reason Jackie decided she had finally had enough and she wanted me out. My girlfriend Nic had been part of our high school group of friends, and we found ourselves working together at the bank. Having overnight stays at Nic's wasn't uncommon, as we would go out at night and go to work together the next day. One night when I innocently called and asked Jackie if I could stay at Nic's house overnight, Jackie told me it was time to move out. 'If you never want to be home then you should move out for good,' she calmly advised me.

Once the words were spoken a part of me just wanted out. I'd never considered leaving home. I was scared shitless of being alone, but now I wondered if this opportunity had been handed to me.

I may have believed I was an adult but, in reality, I was only 17 and had never been out on my own before. I didn't know what I was going to do, so my friend Nic assured me I could stay with her and her parents until I sorted myself out. We were both fairly certain the whole thing would blow over in the morning, and that whatever was upsetting Jackie could be rectified by a night's sleep. I rang my friend Debbie and she agreed to come with me the next morning when I returned home, but when we arrived there was no sign of my stepmum, dad or sisters. I had no idea what to do, so I filled a few garbage bags with my possessions and Debbie took me back to Nic's place.

To this day my stepmum swears it was my decision to leave, that she had never intended for me to take her seriously and that if I had asked her she would have told me to stay.

I spent a few weeks with Nic and her parents then moved in with an older friend. Weeks turned to months, then Dad and Jackie told me they were moving to Queensland and said I could go with them. I did go, but I only lasted about six months before I wanted to go back to Canberra. I had felt even more alone in Queensland away from John and my friends: they had become my family too and I needed to be with them more than my real family.

When I returned to Canberra I moved into a flat with John. It seemed like the perfect solution. I loved him very much, and now we could truly be together. I was the first of my friends to have a proper adult relationship and I felt like I was truly living my best life – at least at first. As they say, the honeymoon often doesn't last.

13. CHAOS

There's no such thing as a perfect state of balance in life. It's more like walking on a tightrope where you're constantly balancing.

– ADYASHANTI

If I am honest, it shouldn't have been a surprise that things turned bad so quickly. My relationship with John had always been chaotic. He was a drinker and loved to hang out with his mates, taking drugs during his frequent partying weekends. I rarely drank alcohol and never took drugs, even the soft kinds, so anyone could see we were ill-suited from the start, but somehow we thought it was all going to work out and I set about creating a home for us. It wasn't easy: we ended up having to move quite a few times into dingy flats in Queanbeyan, on the New South Wales border of Canberra, known for its low rents and even lower housing quality.

Back then Queanbeyan had a reputation for being Canberra's poor cousin. It was little more than a country town really, and I don't think much about it has changed even now. There isn't much there save a ton of pubs and clubs and a lot of working-class people trying to struggle through. It seemed to attract people from many of the other smaller country towns that surrounded the ACT, people who couldn't quite afford the price of living in the much more well-appointed suburbs of Canberra. At first I wasn't sure I would fit in, but after a short while it became home and I found some kind of kinship with these other displaced people, all trying to find somewhere safe and secure where they could finally start their real lives.

61

As scary as life was out on my own, it was also the first time I felt I had some semblance of control in my life. I got to choose what was best for me rather than being at the mercy of adults who often made poor, ill-thought-out decisions I had absolutely no say in. Admittedly, not all of my choices were the best ones either, but they were *my* choices and at that time of my life it seemed like that was all that mattered. Not that this was the life I would have chosen if I had been presented with any better options, but what options did I have?

I felt as though I had been abandoned by my family at the age of 17. Mum was living in Bathurst in New South Wales with her beautiful new husband Brian, and Dad, Jackie and Shannon were in Brisbane in Queensland. While I kept in regular contact with Mum and Dad, the cost of interstate phone calls at the time was high and they were saved for special times. I felt alone when I was with my family because I wanted my friends but then I felt alone when I was with my friends when they had their families, so I clung more tightly to the only thing I could: John.

At least in Queanbeyan I had Debbie and her parents, who had become my stability and my family. Even with my changing circumstances, Debbie and I remained best friends and seamlessly slipped into each other's lives no matter what else was changing around us.

I can see that I was surprisingly resilient, moving around, losing and gaining family and friends in unpredictable ways. I think it was because I always had the attitude that we have to make mistakes in order to know how to avoid them in the future, which is how we grow and develop toughness and wisdom. There will always be days when we struggle just to make it through the next few minutes, the next few days, weeks, months and sometimes years, but we always come out the other side knowing more about ourselves than when we went in.

I do sometimes wish I had made it a little easier on myself or learned my lessons a little bit sooner, because living with John was far from a healthy experience. His drinking, aggressive behaviour and disrespect towards me were seemingly not enough for me to realise that I really would be better off without him. Even when we did reach breaking point and separate, which occurred at least once a year, we always ended up getting back together. I can't explain why I always felt the need to return to him; perhaps it was the same thing that kept me within that mean group of girls back in high school or made me want to return to my dad's house even when I knew the atmosphere was unpredictable, or why I didn't tell anyone about the abuse and fear I suffered when Roger got violent. All of those things were part of it.

If I am honest, I think the real reason behind all of my silences and acceptance of the state of my life was because I feared that if I really had to deal with these things I would have to deal with them alone. I would have to truly look at myself and my circumstances and the things that had and were happening around me and make some real hard and potentially irrevocable choices. When I was in the midst of the chaos, fighting and laughing with John and enjoying the good times as well as the bad, I didn't have time to think or examine my life or my past or really think about the future. The present, no matter how difficult, still seemed safer to me.

But it wasn't safer. In fact, it was probably one of the least-safe situations of my entire life. When John drank he got cranky, and when he got cranky the chances were he would lose his temper entirely and that could potentially lead to him taking his frustration out on me: pushing me around, sometimes a smack or punch to the head. If I was particularly unlucky I copped a severe beating. It sounds awful and it was, but at the time I normalised it. After all, it wasn't as though I wasn't used to violence and, really, what were the alternatives?

What hurt me most wasn't the violence; it was the words John said to me, words that couldn't be taken back once they were spoken. More damaging than physical violence, John's words were more often than not the catalyst for me to finally get angry enough to leave and swear never to return.

I did keep returning, though, for years, and it never really got any better. I would lie to myself and promise that at some point it would get better, and I repressed most of my memories of the violence and degradation. Even now I resist setting down any of the details on paper. When you live a life that's full of chaos and violence, your barometer of what is acceptable and what isn't becomes distorted. You accept and become accustomed to behaviours and events other people would have nightmares about. Not only was I regularly at risk of physical violence, but more than once I was unwillingly made complicit in John's criminal acts and highly risky behaviour.

I recall a particular day when one of John's more dubious acquaintances turned up at our apartment with a huge smile on his face. He was wearing one of those thin plastic-looking windbreakers, and it was bulging in a very odd way as he breezed into our flat. I immediately suspected what he had under there, but before I could form the words to tell him to get that stuff out of our place he had unzipped his jacket and several bags of tightly packed marijuana spilled to the floor. I looked at it disbelievingly, wondering where the hell he had got it all from. While I never participated in drug taking and rarely drank alcohol, just by association I constantly placed myself at risk and most of this was happening in my own house.

Years later as I began the journey to understanding myself I came across the word 'co-dependent'. Funnily enough the word isn't used that much these days, perhaps because it's been outdated by better terms such as 'relationship addiction', but I still find the word relevant. In simple terms it means one person allows another person to make the decisions in their relationship and effectively becomes a silent companion for fear of rejection or violence and low self-esteem. This makes it almost impossible for the passive partner to set boundaries, because they are so busy meeting the needs of their partner there is no time left to explore or tend to their own needs or wants.

Looking back, I was firmly entrenched in a co-dependent relationship: I was fearful of rejection, of John leaving me and being alone. On the outside I smiled and laughed and most people liked me, but internally I struggled with low self-esteem and self-hatred for being so weak. I convinced myself that I didn't deserve someone better.

Ironically, I was quite attractive and often found myself fending off advances from members of the opposite sex, mostly because I knew if John ever suspected I was interested in another man he would not be happy. As a result I lived in a constant state of anxious hypervigilance, always trying to prevent violence that I had no way of preventing, never mind predicting. By the time I was 20 I had been hospitalised with stomach ulcers. I overheard the doctors in the hospital talking about how they had never seen anything like this in a person of my age, but this was my life, and with my messed-up sense of self-esteem I didn't think it was that bad.

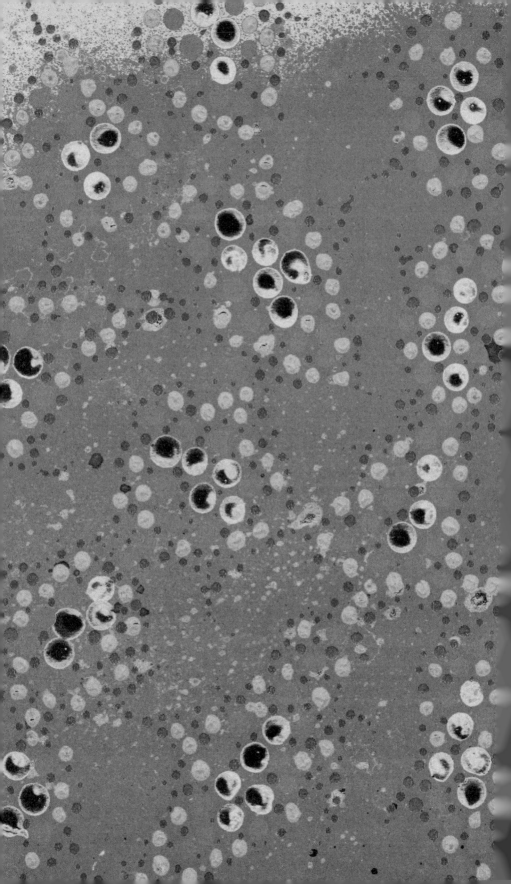

14. SHATTERING THE GLASS

That awkward moment when
you have your running shoes
on, but you just can't run.

– UNKNOWN

The relationship between John and me was difficult enough, but there was one thing that made it even worse: a particular arsehole of a man I'll refer to as 'Gavin'. He was an acquaintance who seemed determined to cause as much drama between me and John as was humanly possible, and appeared to feed on the anxiety and violence he caused in our relationship. He would arrive at our apartment and convince John to go out, take drugs and drink too much, knowing how that affected John and our relationship.

The result was always an argument, with me pleading or yelling at John to stay home and to not get drunk or stoned because a drunk John was dangerous to both of us. As we argued Arsehole Gavin would sit there watching us, smirking because we all knew exactly how the argument would end: with him and John walking out the door together, leaving me alone and fuming.

I gave John everything I had to give. If anyone deserved loyalty, wasn't that me? Wasn't I the one who put up with the occasional floggings, his infidelity, his excessive drug and alcohol use because I wished so desperately to be everything John wanted and needed but could never make the grade?

I was so fed up with this arsehole and the way John deferred to him that finally I declared enough was enough: the next time Arsehole Gavin arrived I was going to put my foot down, and so I did. Arsehole Gavin thought it was hilarious when I declared that if John wanted to be with Gavin so much then they should go and live together. Gavin thought this was a great idea and goaded me on, telling John how happy he'd be to share a place with him. 'I'll even help you move out,' he assured John as he grinned at me with a look of complete triumph. I was incensed. I didn't really want John to leave, but I had been forced into a corner thanks to the arsehole egging us both on. I told John to go, that I would be fine on my own, but the truth was I was more scared of being alone than I was of living this life full of violence and drugs – and both John and the arsehole knew it.

At the time we lived in a flat on the second floor that had a balcony overlooking the car park. Arsehole Gavin and John were down in the car park packing John's things into Arsehole's car, at the same time throwing insults up at me. Watching them with a mixture of horror and rising desperation, I realised that John was really doing it: he was leaving me for this arsehole! I backed into the flat, trying to hush the silent screaming in my head and feeling utterly desperate inside. Suddenly a very large, hideous glass-covered print that John had bought caught the corner of my eye. I had always hated that print, which looked like someone had vomited on canvas after ingesting a particularly rancid kebab. In that moment the picture represented all that was shit in my life, all the things I put up with and all the awfulness John had brought into my life.

I picked up the print and carried it to the balcony. I felt as though I was watching myself through someone else's eyes as I walked to the railing, leaned out and dropped the print, glass frame and all, over the side of the building towards where John and Arsehole were standing. I calmly advised Arsehole to 'Catch!' as the glass frame sailed downwards. Ever the coward, Arsehole Gavin ran for cover seconds before the frame hit the ground and shattered into a thousand pieces of splintered glass. John hardly even moved as the picture exploded so close to him that glass flew up and rained down in tiny, glitter-like shards in the car park, and just stood there staring up at me in perplexed disbelief.

I may have looked calm as I stood on that balcony watching Arsehole and John hurriedly get into their car and drive away, but inside I was wracked with fear: after this little performance I was definitely going to be living on my own forever! However, the turmoil inside me didn't show as I calmly returned inside, and it was only once I was behind the safety of the closed door that I collapsed to the floor in a hysterical mess. It's funny that even though you feel your life has just fallen apart and your heart has been broken into 1,000 pieces, like the glass all over the car park below, you can control your breakdown enough so that no one else can hear it happen.

Something that strikes me later in life is why no one came to see what was happening. There were 30 or more flats in that building and we all shared the same driveway, with the balconies facing the car park below. People must have heard what was happening, but no one came to investigate and no one came to see if I was okay. No one even rang the cops. Were people too scared to intervene, or did they not care? I suppose I shouldn't have been that surprised, because no one had cared when John was beating the crap out of me either.

That should have been the end of us, of John and me, as a couple, but I am unhappy to say that once again my fear of being alone convinced me to sort it out with John and welcome him back with contritely loving arms. The only silver lining was that after that frame shattered beside him Arsehole kept his distance and was somewhat more respectful towards me.

The months marched on and I came out of my teenage years and entered my 20s, still trapped in a cycle of violent break-ups and tearful reunions over and over like a record that constantly skips on the same verse of a well-worn song. I simply didn't know how to take the damn record off.

Finally, after another bad argument with John I decided I could no longer endure the pain that separation with him caused me, nor could I hope for a happy reunion where we would stay together safe forever. Loss and abandonment, struggle, violence and neglect had always been what my life was defined by, and there was only one way I could think of to escape it. I went through the house and took every tablet and drug I could find, determined to end my suffering there and then. I woke up the next morning feeling worse than I had ever felt in my life, hung over and dehydrated but alive – and pissed off. Seeing nothing else for it, I picked myself up, dusted myself off and went to work.

Aunty Lynda had recently moved to Canberra for work, so having her living so close by was a life-saving moment. It had been one of the worst days of my life, and that afternoon while visiting Aunty Lynda I confided in her about what I had done the night before. Lynda didn't lecture me or tell me I was stupid, or even that she understood. She simply asked me to look after her daughter Tia for the next few days. Lynda knew that while I had Tia in my care I would never think of doing anything as stupid as I had just tried to do. I loved Tia like she was my daughter, and Lynda rightly banked on that to get me through the next few days until I was back to some semblance of sanity. It's not that I completely came to my senses, as John and I had many more tearful reconciliations and violent break-ups over the next few years, but I began to realise that more than my physical health was being impacted by my relationship with John. My mental health was suffering, too.

15. ONE OF THE GOOD GUYS

Hope is being able to see that there
is light despite all of the darkness.

– DESMOND TUTU

My relationship with John was tumultuous, violent and co-dependent in the worst ways. Of course, you can't see that while you're experiencing it but occasionally you do glimpse other possibilities, other ways your life could be.

Chris was that for me, a man I thought could offer me something better, could treat me better and be better. Chris was, I believed, one of the good guys: he didn't drink much alcohol, had a great bunch of friends and never did drugs. I was 20 years old when we met, but I felt like a love-struck teenager the moment I first laid eyes on him. Unfortunately, he worked in the same place as John and they were colleagues, if not friends, so I knew that anything romantic with him was an impossibility for both of us. I couldn't resist him entirely, though, so I forged a friendship, nothing more really than a friendly acquaintanceship. It wasn't difficult, and Chris soon became part of our social circle and I saw him regularly at social events and nights out.

John often abandoned me at these parties, going off to drink with his mates, and I found myself standing around listening to Chris tell us all about his favourite football team or his job or just mindless chit-chat. Whatever he said seemed extremely interesting to me regardless of the subject matter, and I knew I was getting more and more infatuated with every conversation. Chris was smart and funny and he listened when I spoke. After being treated as though I barely mattered within my relationship with John, who could blame me for fantasising about something better? However, it was just that, a fantasy – until, well, it wasn't.

After yet another alcohol-fuelled argument John and I broke up again, only this time it felt different from all the other times. This time I didn't feel desperate or sad because I kept thinking about Chris and that maybe, just maybe, this was my chance with him. When John left he took our shared car, and I had no option but to use the poor excuse for public transport that Queanbeyan offered its residents. I was forced to walk a lot, including when I did the shopping or had to go to and from work.

One day I found myself walking down the road with some groceries when Chris appeared out of nowhere and offered me a lift home. I gratefully accepted and got into his car. He asked if I wanted to go straight home and I told him I didn't. I don't know why I said that but it was true, and he smiled and we ended up on a drive together taking in the sights and chatting about our lives. In that car I was afforded a glimpse into a world where nice blokes treated women like they were actual human beings, with thoughts and feelings and ideas. I started to think: maybe this is how women should be treated. Maybe this is how *I* should be treated.

Our friendship grew from an acquaintanceship and blossomed into a very covert romantic relationship. I was not back together with John, but I understood it wouldn't be wise to let him know I was seeing someone else, particularly someone he worked with. Chris agreed to keep our feelings quiet but, still, for the first time it felt like I had a real boyfriend and not a fellow combatant. Keeping the friendly pretence, Chris invited me to see a movie with him and a mate who was visiting him. At first I wished it had been just me and Chris, but Chris said he liked that he had the chance to show me off to his mate and I felt really flattered that he had told his friend how much he liked me. Both Chris and his friend were complete gentlemen and treated me like a lady, opening doors, paying for my movie popcorn and talking and listening to me like I mattered.

It was eye opening and sadly something I could never recall experiencing before, but I believed it was definitely something I could get used to. 'Maybe,' a tiny voice in the back of my head whispered shyly, 'just maybe I did deserve better than what I had settled for with John.'

We continued to keep quiet about the relationship. John and I may have split up, but I knew he could make things awkward and was worried about his temper and unpredictability should he catch wind that I was seeing someone else. I admit I rather liked the clandestine affair between Chris and I, a delicious, exciting secret only the two of us shared . . . until the work party.

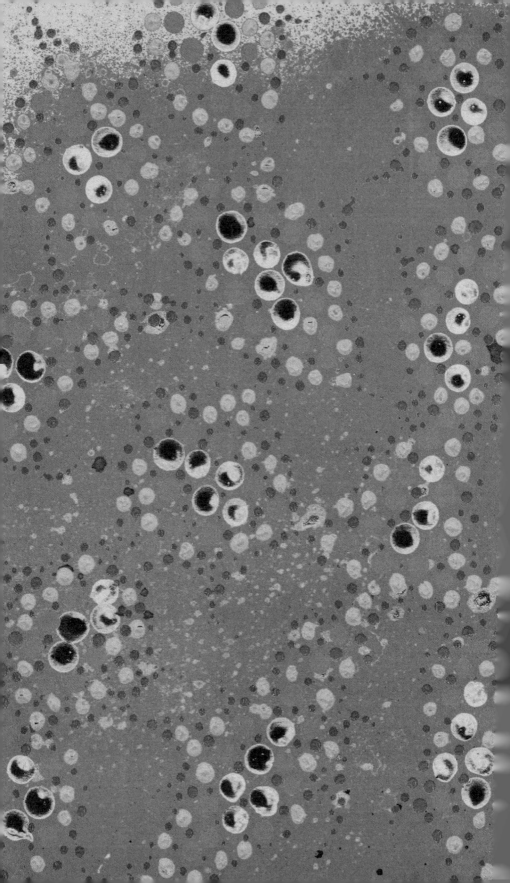

16. 'FOR YOUR OWN SAFETY'

Seriously, when does this shit ever end!

– Unknown

I can see now it was a bad idea from the start, attending a party where both Chris and my ex would be present. It was never going to end well, but Chris and I were both full of confidence and young naivety so we thought we could be discreet and no one would know what we had going on. We were careful, making sure we were never alone together or seen to be overly familiar beyond the friendship most knew we shared. I watched Chris chatting with other people, paying even more attention when other women were talking with him. I quietly smiled to myself, knowing those women didn't have a chance because he was going home with me!

On this night John was drinking heavily, which was the norm for him, but he was also particularly attentive to me and kept close tabs on what I was doing and who I was talking with. This was unusual, because usually as soon as we arrived at any party or social gathering he couldn't wait to head over to the main action of drinking or drug taking. Yet on this night John rarely left me alone and there was only one occasion when Chris and I were able to even sneak a few smiles across the room. I thought we were pretty discreet and we certainly did nothing to arouse suspicion while we were there, but John somehow knew exactly what was going on. Perhaps he knew before he arrived, because someone else had found out about Chris and I and had clued John in on it.

Whatever the reason for John's behaviour, he seemed determined that we were going to get back together and resume our life of chaos. I told him this was not going to happen and left the party, making sure Chris saw that I was leaving and hoping he would meet me at

75

my house soon after. Chris and I had already planned to meet at my place afterwards, and I couldn't wait to get home and finally spend some time with him. The longing created by having him so near and being unable to touch him was making my heart and body ache, and I couldn't wait to be safely in his arms away from the suspicious glares of my crazy ex-boyfriend.

Chris took a while to get to my place. As I waited for him I got increasingly worried that he wasn't coming at all, but when he arrived he told me he had walked there as he had been too drunk to drive and my irritation disappeared. Chris was not only someone who understood that driving drunk was incredibly stupid, but he was also willing to walk in the freezing cold all the way to my place instead just so he could be with me. I thought I had finally found a man who truly cared for me and we immediately fell into bed and quickly fell asleep in each other's arms, sighing with happiness after what I felt had been an almost perfect night. Then my sleep was disturbed by someone hammering violently at my front door.

My heart started racing a million miles an hour. I looked at the alarm clock by my bed in the darkened room. It glowed with the time: 3 am! Who would hammer at my door at 3 am? I looked over at Chris but he was dead to the world, the alcohol he had consumed all night having taken its toll. I don't think a bulldozer would have woken him, because even the loud banging on the door had not caused him to stir.

Of course, I knew who it was who felt they had the right to come barrelling up to my flat in the middle of the night, yelling and shouting at me to let them in, but I wasn't going to let them come in: not tonight. I was not going to let John ruin this perfect night for me or threaten the wonderful man who was snoring peacefully in my bed.

John, drunk and belligerent, kept banging at the door. I knew it was him, and I knew he wasn't going to go away quietly. I was worried that he would wake an angry neighbour and I realised the best thing to do was probably to try to calm him down and get him to leave before he caught Chris in the bedroom. I walked out into the living room, closing the bedroom door securely behind me, and prepared to face John.

As soon as I opened the door John barged inside, heading straight for the bedroom. It's like he knew exactly what had been going on and who was there, and I had no time to try to stop him. I knew then that I had been caught; it was scary, but also a relief. I was willing to face the music because, as fun as the sneaking around had been at first, I really wanted my relationship with Chris to come out. After all, I wasn't with John, I was with Chris, and now I could be open about it.

John was not alone. One of his acquaintances, a particularly sleazy bloke I'll refer to as 'Damian', was with him, and as John pushed his way into the flat Damian grabbed me and pulled me out into the hallway. He slammed the door closed, leaving us both standing out in the stairwell. I was barely dressed, wrapped in a flimsy dressing gown I had hastily put on before opening the door but totally naked beneath, and I felt scared and vulnerable out there on the open landing.

I cried and begged to be let back in, but Damian wasn't going to have a bar of it. He was there to back up John and help him teach me a lesson, and was not going to let me go. Behind the closed door I could hear all hell breaking loose. I was terrified for Chris, but the more I struggled and pleaded with Damian to let me go and for John to calm down the more Damian restrained me. 'You don't wanna go in there,' Damian said, leering at me, 'for ya own safety, love.'

I could hear John kicking and belting into Chris and desperately wanted to help him. I struggled and Damian took the opportunity to grab at and grope me right on the stairwell as my ex-boyfriend was inflicting unknown harm on my current boyfriend. I could do very little to protect myself from this mongrel, who had his hands all over me and under my dressing gown. I tried swiping his disgusting mitts away but he was relentless.

I think I was in that stairwell for at least 10 minutes, terrified for Chris more than myself even as I was being sexually assaulted 'for my own safety'. I never told anyone about what happened in the stairwell that night, partly because of the shame I felt allowing it to happen but mostly because it was, essentially, unremarkable: just further confirmation that I was nothing. No one was there to help me, and that alone proved that I deserved what I got. How could someone as worthless and weak as me ever be good enough for someone like Chris, and why would he ever want to see me again after I had led John right to him?

In the months that followed Chris and John made up and continued to work together as mates, the way men so often can, and I ended up back with John – almost like that was a bargain they had made between them. I must have agreed to it, must have accepted John back and given up on any real relationship with Chris, but I don't remember consciously doing so. It's just what happened, and I accepted it.

17. PHOTO

Dodging a close call or tight spot felt like barely avoiding a horrible accident and winning the lottery all at the same time – and I felt surges of relief and exhilaration.

– CHARLIE SPILLERS

Over the next few months as John and I continued our cycle of break-ups and recriminations and seemingly inevitable reconciliations Chris and I also hooked up, tempting fate for it all to happen again. We were almost caught a few times, the closest call being when we were in bed one night at Chris's place and there was a knock on the door. My heart stopped and my ears pricked up as John yelled at Chris to come out and have a drink with him. I signalled to Chris to be quiet and laid in bed paralysed with fear, not knowing what was going to happen next. Memories of a not-so-distant past came flooding back to me.

Chris's housemate Jack answered the door. We could hear John's voice bold as brass, and him drunk as a skunk saying he wanted to say hello to Chris. Chris was just one closed door away, in his bed with me.

'Hey, mate, good to see you,' Jack said smoothly. 'Chris has got company right now, so maybe not the best time to be visiting.'

'Yeah, does he?' John slurred. 'Who's he with?' There was a pause and I heard John ask with slight menace: 'Anyone I know?'

Jack laughed, and damn if it didn't sound completely genuine – not even a touch of nervousness even though he knew exactly who I was and exactly how John would react if he found me there with Chris. 'Nah, mate, someone he picked up at the club, I think. You ain't one of those blokes who is going to go and spoil a fella's lucky night, are ya?'

John agreed he was definitely not one of those blokes, and after a few more moments of casual chit-chat he left and I heard Jack sigh with relief. I remember sitting in the darkness of Chris's room after John left, listening to Jack start up the TV in the living room and thinking to myself that I had yet again put both myself and Chris and even his poor flatmate in danger. My relationship with John was dangerous, not just for me but for anyone else I got entangled with. For some reason I couldn't see a life where John didn't hang around and threaten me whether we were together or not, so I couldn't keep putting other people in danger. I left Chris's house, and once again got back together with John.

In most relationships where there is family violence there are also good times, the times you try to think about the most in order to justify why you stay. John and I did have good times and I wasn't always sad and scared. We had good friends, we spent time camping and we probably ate more barbecues than meals inside. Our life wasn't that bad, except when it was that bad: that's how these relationships survive. Perhaps if there had been less of the good times I would have truly been able to leave, but those memories always gave me something to cling to, in hope that life with John could get better.

Finally, the constant rollercoaster of life with John had worn thin and I was determined I was not going to be tricked, frightened or tempted to get back with him again. Nothing was going to change, and I knew I wanted to be with Chris in a proper relationship. I left John for good and began seeing Chris again, and this time it felt different. We talked about a possible future together and started to act like we were in a proper relationship, but we were still cautious and didn't flaunt our relationship.

We had been together like this for a few months and I really thought my life had changed. John was in the rear-view mirror, and what lay ahead was clear skies and a proper relationship with a man who treated me as though I was worthwhile. I went to Brisbane to spend Christmas with my family, leaving Chris back in Queanbeyan. There I was early one morning having a lazy sleep in at Dad and my stepmum's when I realised I had not had my period in quite a while. I started doing the sums, counting the days since my last period. Holy shit! I raced to tell Jackie what I suspected, and within hours a doctor confirmed my pregnancy.

After finding out I was pregnant I rang Chris, knowing this was not going to be the phone call he expected. We had been taking precautions, but like everything else in life they were not 100 per cent reliable. I had a little human growing inside me and I was scared. I had not fallen pregnant on purpose and it was as big a shock to me as anyone else, but as I made the call a little part of me dared to hope Chris would be up to the challenge of fatherhood and would be happy to fully commit to sharing his life with me and our child. I even dared to dream that maybe I was good enough after all.

Chris was understandably stunned by my news, and it took him a few moments to find the words to respond. When he did, though, I knew all my hopes of a happy outcome for the three of us were dashed. 'Melinda, it's not the right time for us to think about having a baby,' he said seriously. His tone told me that he was not going to be talked around or convinced otherwise. I could have tried harder to convince him, I suppose, but while growing up I had seen what having an unexpected pregnancy had done to my parents' relationship and I didn't want Chris and I to end up like Mum and Dad, so I went along with what he wanted and allowed him to make the decision for me.

Surprisingly, it was Jackie who came to my aid. Our time apart seemed to have strengthened our relationship and she became a lifeline for me in those few days, arranging an appointment for me to have a termination the following week. I don't remember much about those days waiting to terminate my baby, but I do recall going to Sea World with my sisters. There were so many rides that had signs warning pregnant women to avoid them, and they reminded me of my pregnancy every time I read the friendly block lettering. I didn't go on those rides, because at least for the time left for me I wanted to act like a good mother, protecting and caring for the child inside me.

I had a professional and very expensive photo taken of me feeding a dolphin. Most people looking at that photo just see a smiling young woman in a short shirt and shorter shorts feeding a dolphin, but what

I see is a photo of a lost little girl hiding her guilt, fear and hurt behind a smile as inauthentic as the dolphins that surround her. It is also the only photo I had of that child. Even if she wasn't perceivable in it, I know she was there. I treasured that photo for many years without telling anyone the significance of it.

18. THE RULE OF THREE

As part of me disappeared,
no one noticed.

– Unknown

Walking into the clinic on the day of the termination, I wondered how my mum felt all those years ago when she was 17 and approached that backyard abortionist in an effort to be rid of me and the problems I represented. I was 20 and only a bit older than my mum had been, and I was doing this in a clinic staffed with medical professionals and being picked up a few hours later by someone who would take me home and care for me. My mum had none of that and she had bravely faced it, and so could I.

I had to see a counsellor prior to the procedure and had read somewhere that they would decide whether or not I was emotionally fit enough to have the termination, so with all my strength I tried not to cry. I was angry at Chris as I sat through the counsellor's appointment without him: angry that he wasn't having to experience this or be responsible in any way for the life he had helped create. At least my dad had gone with Mum when she had faced this. As the counsellor spoke I made the decision to let the anger go, as it would do no one any real good. I replaced it with a determination that after I left that place I would return home to Queanbeyan with my head held high. I would survive this and I would go on.

Not with Chris, though: I already knew there would be no future with him. Our few telephone conversations over the past weeks had been wary and strained, and it was obvious he had no interest in continuing on with me even though he hadn't said the actual words.

I went to see him when I returned home. He hadn't contacted me after the termination and I had heard nothing from him since

I had gone back to Queanbeyan, but part of me had to see him face to face to know for sure it was truly over. He ushered me into his room, standing as far away from me as he could get, and distantly and politely told me we needed a break and that was that. The words had now been said.

I walked out of Chris's room and past Jack, who was sitting shamefaced in the lounge room. We had become good friends while I was seeing Chris, and I couldn't look at him as I said goodbye because I knew I would see pity reflected in his eyes and that would be the part where I came undone. I walked out that door and to my car determined that no one would have the chance to see the devastation I was feeling. It was the saddest and most dejected I had ever felt in my life.

Thoughts of what I had done and the baby I would never have darkened my thoughts on many a sleepless night and were often followed by equally dark days. Sometimes I thought about it often, while at other times months or years would go by without me dwelling on the child I had lost. I would ask those terrible questions that could never be answered. What would my child have been like? Could I have been a good enough mum to raise a child on my own if I had made a different decision? I also wondered about the life I robbed from my baby: what kind of life could it have been? If my mother and father had been successful in their attempts to get rid of me would I have ended up somewhere else in another life, happier, sadder, or not ever have existed at all?

This started me thinking about the lives we lived, and part of me started to think that maybe this life we have, maybe it isn't all there is, that my baby would go on to have another existence, that our souls are eternal and the bodies we inhabit only temporary. I couldn't quite articulate this thought in my early 20s, but it was a belief that started to develop and formulate as I moved further through my Dreaming and into a sense of who I was, now and before.

At the time I was only in my early 20s and still very much a child who believed in happy endings, so I longed for Chris to take me back. I believed he felt something for me too. We had a habit of somehow constantly finding ourselves in each other's orbit, such as the time a girlfriend and I decided to attend a local bachelors and spinsters ball. We were out looking fabulous when who should be there when I turned around but Chris, with his new girlfriend and some of his mates. I resented Chris for that, for moving on so quickly from what we had had together.

The irony of this eluded me at the time. During my time with Chris I so easily ran back to John each time things ended, my fear of being alone always overcoming my good sense. I did it again that night, though thankfully not by running back to John but by hooking up with one of Chris's new flatmates.

Don't get me wrong: it may have started out as a bit of revenge, but Chris's flatmate Anthony was a lovely guy so I started seeing him for real and developed an affection for him. He was never going to be someone I loved, but he was certainly someone I really liked and he was enjoyable to spend time with. I never considered how this might have affected him or whether his feelings for me were deeper than those I had for him. All I thought about was myself and how nice it was to have this relationship right in front of Chris's nose. It was justice, I felt, if it made Chris feel uncomfortable. He deserved it.

One night while I was visiting Anthony, Chris took the opportunity to ask me for a private chat. Surprisingly, Anthony agreed. In hindsight, I think they may have talked about this prior to my arrival because it was all so grown up and amicable. I went to Chris's room, where we sat on his bed. He shared with me his sorrow for what he had done and apologised for how he had treated me. He retrieved the birthday and Valentine cards I had given to him at different times over the past years and sat beside me, so close we were almost touching, as he read out the words I had written to him. Somehow I held myself together as he looked at me after reading each heartfelt message, words that expressed my love for him and the hope of a future together. I had no such mementos because he had never given or written me anything during our entire time together.

It was then I realised that what I thought I had with Chris was not what I thought it was at all. All the shit that had happened to me since I had met him, juggling him and John with their needs, their jealousies and their insecurities and lack of commitment: all of it was toxic. None of it was coming from a place of love or nourishment or nurture. It was all damaging. I sensed something big in me shift, my first glimpse of what I later understood to be one of the major karmic laws that govern our actions. Spiritual people call it the Rule of Three or Threefold Law. It determines that whatever we put out into the world comes back to us three times over, so if you send good stuff out then good stuff comes back, and if you send bad stuff out then duck for cover because the shit storm is coming and it's going to be a bad day.

My constant back and forth with John and my need to get back with Chris even though he had hurt me so badly: none of this was me sending good intentions into the world no matter how I might justify things. I had to change the way I was living my life, and the universe was not going to let me have a moment's rest until I did.

I let Chris go, a mature and reasonable decision, but I was still seeing Anthony. He was a good guy, and I now realise I was still not willing to be totally on my own. I had not learned the full lesson that karma had been trying to teach me so she came back into my life with all guns blazing.

It happened, as these things so often do, unexpectedly and in the middle of the night. A few weeks later I was asleep in Anthony's bed, as I had taken to staying with him some nights. I felt calm and safe beside him, as though all the craziness of the last few years was finally over. But, of course, it wasn't, and that night it came back hammering on Anthony's door like a vengeful case of déjà vu. I woke with my heart almost bursting from my chest, momentarily thinking I had simply had a nightmare, a flashback to the times John had crashed into my life. The hammering had not stopped when my eyes opened and I realised it was really happening, so I climbed out of bed and peeked out the window to see John's car parked out the front of the house.

I wish I could say I was surprised, but part of me wasn't. It didn't matter that we had been separated for months or that John had no way of knowing I would be at that address. Somehow, part of me knew that he was always destined to find me, that my life with him was not over – not yet. There he was pounding on the door in another drunken rage, and yet again I had placed someone besides myself in danger.

Fearing John would break in and hurt more innocent people, I hurried out to the living room, opened the door and tried to calm him but he was ranting and raving and beyond reason. I was resigned to my fate and was, once again, totally on my own.

As he turned to me I realised I was barely dressed: in my distress I had only had time to throw on a thin T-shirt before answering the door. I was wearing nothing else, no coat and no underwear. Seeing me like that seemed to set off a whole new range of emotions in John, and he grabbed me and pulled me out of the house and towards the car. He was so strong and his action so unexpected I was unable to put up any kind of resistance.

Queanbeyan in winter is cold, and that night was no different as John dragged me across the frosted front lawn and shoved me into his new Brock Commodore. As he walked around to get in the driver's side I tried to make a run for it, but he was too quick and caught me and dragged me back to the passenger seat by my arm. He sat on me, pinning me with his weight as he slammed the car door shut and then locked it, before sliding over to the driver's seat and starting the car while still holding me down with his left arm.

Drunk and angry, John took off like a bat out of hell, squealing tyres and burning rubber as we drove away. I was terrified. As we drove I realised John was heading out around the back of Queanbeyan using the back roads, dark and isolated and empty but for the occasional reflective eyes of a startled kangaroo on the side of the road. I begged him to slow down: he must have been doing more than 200 kilometres per hour, and I knew hitting a kangaroo at those speeds would be fatal to us and the animal. He refused to slow down, recklessly taking turns and skidding dangerously on the ice-covered back roads.

'Please, John,' I begged. 'Please just stop. We can talk about it.'

John just stared ahead, his jaw clenched and his eyes wild as he seemingly drove even faster around each corner. My head banged against the side window as he righted the car, never slowing so much as one kilometre as he manoeuvred the car through the darkened night.

'Please, please, *stop!*' I cried.

Suddenly, John pulled on the handbrake. The car began spinning, a sickeningly high-speed circle that felt as slow as molasses and as fast as the blink of an eye. I watched the blackened bushland blur past my windows like some demonic carousel. How we didn't hit the tree that quickly loomed in front of us I will never know.

It's weird what goes through my mind at a time like this. There was a good chance I was going to die, either from a car crash or because John was going to kill me with his drunken bare hands, but at the time I was more worried about the damage his reckless driving was doing to the car. We shared repayments on that car, and I remember thinking how stupid it was for him to damage it as we would never be able to afford a new one.

When the car finally stopped spinning John told me to get out. His voice was low and quiet but seemed all the more dangerous because of that. We were in the middle of nowhere in the dark, I was barely dressed and it was around minus 3 degrees Centigrade outside. I made no move to leave the car because, as dangerous as he was, I knew the cold and the elements on that freezing Queanbeyan night would be more likely to kill me and I had survived his rage before. Sensing my reluctance, John leaned over and pushed my car door open then, with a mighty shove, he pushed me out onto the cold, hard ground.

'Get in front of the car, Melinda, because I am going to run you over.'

I shook my head in dazed bewilderment. What was he saying? He couldn't be serious, but his eyes were hard and his face had no humour in it. 'I'm not doing that,' I said, scrambling to my feet and backing away from the car, the sharp bitumen on the road cutting at my soft bare feet. 'Please just let me back in the car. It's cold and . . . Please, John.'

'Yeah, but you don't want to be with me, do ya, Melinda?'

'Take me home, John, and I will stay with you, I promise,' I cried, knowing it was my only hope of avoiding being left for dead on the side of the road. John considered that for a moment and then, to my utter surprise, he nodded and I literally dived through the open door as he remained staring straight ahead.

We drove back to my flat without saying a word to each other, breaking the speed limit the entire journey. Once we were inside John decided to ensure I kept my promise of staying with him by lying across the front door for the rest of the night. There was only one door out of the apartment and that was it, so I was trapped inside.

And so our life of chaos continued.

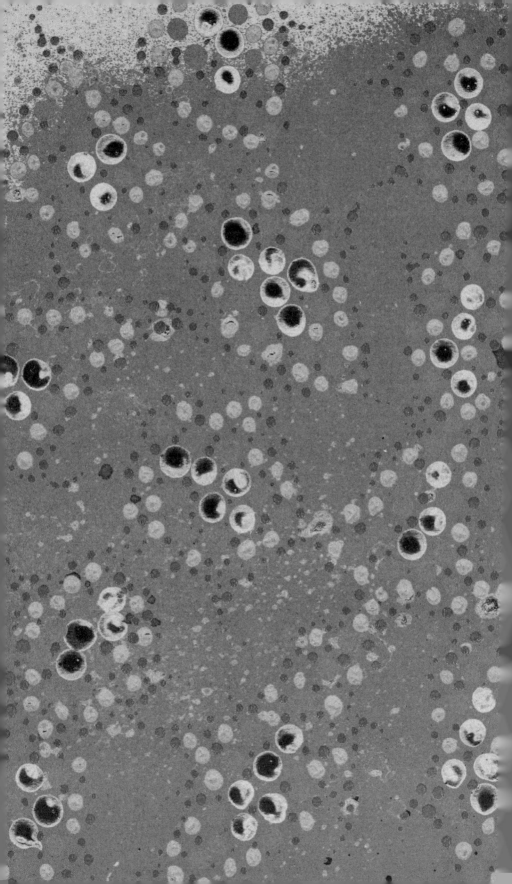

19. STARTING TO HEAL

*Instead of saying 'I'm damaged,
I'm broken . . .' say 'I'm healing, I'm
rediscovering myself, I'm starting over.'*

– HORACIO JONES

John moved into my flat but, despite his presence, I felt totally alone. Lynda had moved to Brisbane and I didn't think anyone would care what was happening to me or how unhappy I was, so I told no one. If something in me hadn't broken I could have walked out. I had lost whatever strength I had regained during my time away from John and fell right back into our old life.

However, I was not quite as alone as I had felt myself to be. My relationship with my mum had slowly grown, and although she had since moved even further away to Townsville we talked regularly. She had long since recognised that my relationship with John was dangerous and toxic and spent hours trying to convince me to leave him and go to stay with her. I wasn't able to do it no matter how much I knew she was right.

Mum tried other ways to remove John. She rang his work and complained about him to his manager, hoping to get him fired. She had some friends of hers accuse him of stealing, hoping to get him arrested, and she thought about dobbing him into the cops about the drugs in our flat except she realised that any raid would likely end up with me being taken into custody too, so she abandoned that plan.

In desperation she even started to plan another one of her insane assassination attempts. This time her plan was to hire someone to kill John, effectively and permanently removing him from my life. Of course, the assassination attempts never actually eventuated, and I don't know if she thought better of it or it wasn't easy to find a qualified hitman hanging around in the ACT. For whatever reason, John remained very much alive and in my life.

Mum's more well-considered effort to get me to leave was to offer to buy me a car. I changed jobs regularly and had always found myself in sales, and I really needed a car as getting to work was difficult without transportation. John and I shared a car, but that really meant I got to use it when he decided I could. Whenever we had an argument he would take the car and leave me stranded. It was part of the power and control he had over me, and he loved to use it.

Mum's offer of a car was a good one and I knew my relationship with John was not healthy for me but, still, I couldn't agree to leave him. I was just so worn down and convinced I was trapped. Mum relented and bought me a car anyway, and it was having this car that did in its own way lead to me leaving John once and for all. He didn't like that he no longer had the same control over me, and he especially hated that I now had the means to flee when the arguments became too much.

As a result our arguments got even more heated and escalated to violence much more frequently. After one particularly nasty fight my girlfriend Sharron, a hairdresser, noticed a huge lump on my head when she was doing my hair. Sharron and her husband Steve were part of our circle of friends and knew about the violence I was experiencing, but they had felt unable to intervene. On this occasion, though, Sharron decided she was not going to just stand by any longer.

'You are leaving him today, this minute,' she said. I shook my head, but she calmly and determinedly said, 'You can come and stay with us until you sort yourself out, but I can't have you going back there. Steve and I will take care of your stuff.'

In that moment I crumbled: finally, someone else had taken control and I didn't have to be responsible. Sharron and Steve picked up my belongings from my house that afternoon, and that was that: the final parting. After all those years, it was over. I mean, truly over. This was the first time anyone had openly and publicly stood up for me and acknowledged the violence that was happening in my life, and I think John didn't know what to say or do about it.

I promised Sharron and Steve that I would never go back and I was not one to go back on my word, especially when they had put their friendship on the line with John to help me. I owed it to them, and I later realised I owed it to myself. I wonder whether if Sharron hadn't put her foot down that day I would have ever ended it with John myself. It had become a cycle of so many years I don't think I even knew how to break it, but the moment Sharron said I shouldn't go back to John I suddenly saw what my life must have looked like to those around me. I was not invisible; I was not worthless. Knowing that others cared enough about me to intervene acted like some kind of circuit breaker in ways that my mother's warnings or my own sense of dread at returning home never could.

I was free, but I was also alone for the first time in my life. No men; just me. It was hard, but not as hard as I thought it would be. As each day and week passed John faded into the background and my group of friends rallied around me. I noticed how, as John's influence over me disappeared, my friendships re-emerged and strengthened.

Shortly after moving in with Sharron and Steve I decided it was time for some counselling. During my first session with the counsellor she recommended I join a women's group for survivors of domestic violence. I was surprised: I wasn't a victim of domestic violence. That was only for women who were severely abused by their husbands. As I told the counsellor, John and I weren't married and I could have left him at any time. She looked at me silently for a full minute and then asked, 'So, why didn't you?'

The question hit home. For the first time I started to think about what had been keeping me with John despite the violence, verbal abuse, my mother's attempts to separate us and my own fear of him. The fact that I had never thought about this question before spoke volumes about my level of acceptance of violence in my relationships. I had lived with violence for so long I didn't even know it was something you didn't have to put up with: I thought it was just the way people related to each other. I had never felt safe, so unsafe was simply normal, wasn't it?

I found solace and understanding within the group of domestic violence survivors. Each of them had their own experiences, their own trauma, yet they took me under their wings and comforted me and made me start to believe that maybe I had never deserved the abuse or neglect or terror I had experienced throughout my life. I reflected on these women, all of whom had experienced this behaviour since childhood, and made a promise to myself I would not allow my children to be raised in a home that was unsafe and violent. My decision to leave John, whether it was my choice or not, had to be sustained. That chapter of my life was over and was never to be repeated.

One of the women in the group recommended I read a book called *Women Who Love Too Much* (Robin Norwood, Pocket Books, 2008). I wasn't that interested at first – after all, what could I learn from a book that I didn't already know – but as I read each chapter I was more and more amazed by the insights the book provided. I often found myself wondering whether the author had been secretly following me around and writing down my experiences in her words. I could not see any other way she was able to articulate exactly why I accepted violence in my life and why I constantly gave myself unconditionally to undeserving people.

This was the first time I clearly remember dipping my toe into the world of personal development and began to understand who I was and, maybe, just maybe, how I would like my life to be if I had the courage to change it. I also became aware that women, particularly those who have experienced violence, trauma or loss as children, will often struggle to understand their options, never mind make good choices as they go into their adult years. Those women need help and support, just as I did.

At the age of 23 I took the next turn in my Dreaming and started down the path of being that support for other women, as well as for myself. I didn't know how to start, but it seemed this was the plan the universe had been trying to guide me towards. When I listen to spirit and the ancestors around me life becomes so much easier, so I soon found myself working with people who had experienced trauma.

Back in those days social work was not the well-developed profession it now is. Most of the people in the sector came there from other areas, often from lives of difficulty and a desire to make a difference, so my lack of education and qualifications were no barrier to me getting a job. I saw an ad in the paper asking for youth workers for a youth refuge for young women aged 12 to 18 who were escaping family violence and sexual abuse. I had absolutely no youth-work experience or qualifications, but I had the lived experience of someone who had navigated this very road as a teenager and was similar in age and outlook to many of the young girls who needed to use the shelter. It seemed I was a natural, and I felt as though I was truly connecting with these young adults and finding through them a way to heal myself as well.

The manager who ran the refuge, Edith, was an amazing woman. Not only had she been willing to take a chance on me but she became a mentor and friend, introducing me not just to social work but to an equally important and I think often underestimated aspect of healing and self-development: the world of alternative and spiritual healing.

Edith was an expert in such exotic-sounding practices as reiki, chakra balancing, kinesiology and many other modes of energetic healing work. All of these practices work with the body's electromagnetic field, allowing us to connect with our sense of self in spiritual and energetic ways. Reiki uses our energy to focus attention and heal other people's damaged energy fields. It uses our bodies as conduits for the life-giving energy that comes from Mother Nature and feeds us and nurtures our souls.

In order to be a reiki master you have to learn how to balance your chakras, the energy wheels or engines that work through our bodies moving energy throughout our whole system, as well as drawing it from the environment around us. Trying to use reiki healing without having a fully functioning and balanced chakra system will lead to the reiki master using up and depleting their own energy, whereas when they are properly balanced and managed the chakras will help the energy come from the universal spirit all around us, using our bodies simply as instruments to channel and focus that energy to heal others.

When Edith first began explaining these things to me I was unsure what the benefit would be, but I sensed immediately that what she was offering was the right thing for me to be doing. It was energy work and spiritual healing connected with my soul on such a deep and immediate level that I never even thought to question whether it was a viable aspect of the social and physical care we were providing to the girls in the refuge.

I soon began to incorporate these practices into my life, which allowed me to start seeing my past behaviour as not just an outcome of circumstance, but a recurring and foundational pattern in my life. I started to read my energy and look for ways in which I could strengthen areas that left me vulnerable to toxic or violent situations. As my energy improved and self-development progressed I found the idea of being alone less terrifying. I started to enjoy solitude and got to know myself as a person whom I could treat with respect, and as a result my whole life also began to improve.

It was the late 1980s and everything looked shiny and possible. Miniskirts were the style of the day and Madonna was our first choice of music. Everyone who was anyone had root perms, even the fellas, and I was no different. Everything about me was wild and messy, including my hairstyle. I was the embodiment of the decade I was living in as I literally let my hair down and revelled in being young and free. I was free of John, free of violence and free of the ideas that had kept me prisoner for most of my young life, and I was going to dance like no one was watching because I had no one to impress but myself.

20. BECOMING A FAMILY

It's amazing that once you begin to love yourself, love will find you.

– UNKNOWN

Part of my new understanding of self was to acknowledge and let go of my commitment to toxic male relationships. This didn't mean I had to remain alone, although I was becoming more comfortable with the idea of that with each passing day. What it did mean was that I would no longer accept men who didn't treat me with respect and care. I was starting to realise that once I stopped believing I was worthless and started to connect with the true soul of my being, I would start to attract men who felt true and real love for me.

That was the frame of mind I was in when the universe finally gave me the threefold result of my newly good intentions, in the form of a handsome, athletic and confident man named Allen. We met on the dance floor of a disco, which is how most people met in the late 1970s and the 1980s before the rise of internet dating and Tinder apps. Allen was so different from the men in any relationship I'd had previously: he wasn't just a good guy, he was a great man.

I was only in the first baby steps of my spiritual journey, and although I had come a long way from the woman I had been when I had allowed myself to be swept into the relationship with John I was still coming to terms with understanding that I was a valuable, worthwhile human being. I therefore struggled for some time with the normality of my relationship with Allen. I had never experienced normal and had nothing to measure it against: the lack of fighting and violence and the sense that there was safety with this man was all completely foreign to me, and I didn't quite understand how to navigate it. The relationship with John had been destructive but it had been familiar. I knew how it would play out and what to expect, which was very little. With Allen, though, I was on unstable ground. Here was a man who actually seemed to not just want to sleep with me, but love me and be there for me.

Without consciously knowing what I was doing I created reasons to argue with him, because this was the only way I knew how to engage in a relationship: through conflict. They were the only rules I knew. The transition from my past into the present with a caring and loving partner wasn't an easy one to make. There were moments when it was uncomfortable, moments when I was way out of my depth and many times when I thought he was way too good for me, and I held my breath in fear that he would leave me. However, over time and with patience I began to learn how to be 'normal' and live life without chaos and violence. It was a shock to know this was what normal was, that this was how many people lived on a daily basis.

Connecting with spiritual healing and having a deeper knowledge of myself and the universal energy that surrounded me certainly helped me navigate the times. Allen was open to exploring those ideas with me as I progressed from simple energy work into more esoteric and spiritual practices such as tarot reading clairvoyance, discovering that my highly tuned senses as a child were the first embryonic evidence of what was becoming a strong and somewhat reliable ability to see beyond my physical world.

Perhaps it was this healing and connection to the universal spirit, as well as my sense of safety with Allen, that led to me falling pregnant just six months into our romance. I had been told I would never have the opportunity to become pregnant or have children after I had experienced my termination when I was with Chris, but here I was with another life growing inside me.

Allen was as surprised by the news as I was, but his response couldn't have been more different than what I had experienced when I broke the news to Chris. Allen was ecstatic and asked me to marry him right there on the spot. I was delighted, but conflicted. I didn't want him to marry me just because I was pregnant. 'Don't be so silly,' he admonished me when I voiced my hesitation. 'I love you, Melinda.' I truly believed him. Allen had casually talked about us getting married over the past few months but I had jokingly said to him, 'Ask me when you're serious.'

I still didn't know what to do. I wanted to marry Allen and build a life together as much as he seemed to, but I was unsure of my ability to make such a huge decision. I needed to talk to someone, and the first person I thought of was Debbie. While my life had been on the upswing after leaving John, Debbie's last months had been far less rosy. Just a year previously she had been in a stable relationship and with a baby on the way, but then tragedy occurred and her baby had been stillborn. Her relationship with her partner was unable to survive the loss, leaving Debbie alone and devastated. I had made sure I was by Debbie's side during her mourning and the breakdown of her relationship, and although I knew she still felt immense loss I had watched as she had slowly pulled her life back together.

I felt selfish at the thought of announcing that I was being given the very things that had so cruelly been snatched away from Debbie, yet I couldn't imagine not telling her. I had an overwhelming, powerful feeling that no matter what she, and only she, was the person who needed to hear my news. If I have learned nothing else it is that the universe does not work in half measures, and I ignore the warnings and messages it gives me at my own peril. So despite a few reservations I decided to share my news with Debbie.

Debbie and her new partner arrived at our place for a barbecue, and I nervously and with great hesitation told her of my pregnancy. 'I didn't know if I should tell you,' I said, weakly, as tears sprung in Debbie's eyes. I was so caught up in my own guilt I didn't at first realise she was crying – with laughter. She was laughing so hard that I worried she was having a breakdown right in front of me.

As her laughter subsided, she said, 'I'm pregnant too!' I didn't know what to say; her news was so unexpected, even more so than mine. I knew she was happy in her new relationship, but I never imagined she would try for a baby again so soon. She had only been with this bloke for few months. 'Ha! You've only been with Allen for six months yourself,' she reminded me.

We broke out laughing. It was true, and how wonderful for us both. We would be going through our journey towards motherhood together, and I couldn't think of anyone I would have rather faced that journey with.

I may have been unsure about whether or not I wanted to marry Allen, but I was absolutely sure I wanted to become a mother and relished every moment of my pregnancy. Debbie and I swapped advice and supported each other through the morning sickness and strange changes in our bodies. Debbie gave birth first, to a healthy, bouncing boy, and my own bundle of joy followed barely 10 days later: a tiny little 2.3 kilogram girl who graced the world with a full head of black hair.

Shortly after giving birth we were taken to the maternity ward. Full of adrenalin, my baby sleeping quietly beside me, I began to tackle the mountain of paperwork required after the birth of a baby. The first question asked the child's first name. That was easy, as I had already decided on Teniel Louise, a beautiful name that suited my adorable little girl right down to the ground. The second question however, was no so easily dispatched: surname. Allen and I were not married, and although we had spoken about her having Allen's surname the enormity of my child, who came out of my body, having a different name from me was really not going to work. I left the page blank and waited for Allen to arrive at the hospital the following morning.

'Do you still want to marry me?' I asked him as soon as he stepped through the door of the maternity ward. So, as unceremoniously as that, we were engaged and set a date nine months from that day, in 1992, to become a complete and united family: all with the same last name.

21. A NEW DREAMING

Being Aboriginal is a personal journey, and no one has the right to tell us how to do it.

– Mel Brown

Shortly after becoming a family Allen and I started talking about how we could afford our own home. We both wanted to build something that would be suitable for our family. Allen had managed to save up enough for a deposit, but building a house would be expensive and I didn't know how we would get a loan because I was no longer working as I was looking after Teniel. It seemed our hopes of home ownership were beyond our present circumstances.

'Why don't you apply for an Aboriginal housing loan?' my mum casually asked as I was telling her about my exciting plans for a three-bedroom house and concerns that it may be beyond our means to achieve it. I didn't know what she was talking about. Why would I apply for an Aboriginal housing loan? 'Because you are Aboriginal' Mum said in a matter of fact way.

'What?' I replied, truly surprised by such a revelation.

'Are all your cousins Aboriginal?' she asked, still maintaining her casualness and talking as though to a child who was having trouble understanding a basic conversation.

'Yes,' I replied. Of course, I had always known my cousins were Aboriginal; it had just never occurred to me that this meant I too was Aboriginal.

My mum's Aboriginality was something that was never talked about, and I suddenly realised that part of who I was had never been acknowledged, never been understood. Now, in my mid-20s,

I had found a whole other part of myself that had been waiting to be discovered.

Dreaming, the journey we take while walking our lives, has no limits. It can progress both forward and while looking backward. I have a Dreaming as Mel Brown, but within this Dreaming there are many journeys. No journey is better or worse than the next; they are simply the choices we make that send us in different directions, and each direction becomes our Dreaming.

As Mum reminded me that I shared her Aboriginal heritage, I began to take on a new Dreaming. My skin colour is light, but the blood of a Blackfella runs through me. Even though at the age of 24 I had little understanding of what that really meant, somewhere inside I felt a shift as I started to see this as being part of my pure truth. In that moment the hairs on my arms stood up and a chill, or more like a vibration, ran through my entire body as the pure unadulterated truth that genetic memory had always known was consciously discovered.

There was sadness, too, for I didn't have any memories of the stories of my Country or from the old grandparents, aunts and uncles, or of participating in our ancient and sacred ceremonies. I grew up thinking none of these things were connected to me, because I had only ever been connected with my white heritage for my whole life.

Learning of my new other equally important heritage was astounding, but I was careful about who I told or how I shared this information with others. Being Aboriginal was not a celebrated identity throughout Australia and I knew that Aboriginal families had suffered greatly from racism and unjust social and legal policies simply because of being Blackfellas, which was why so many also didn't openly discuss their background. Aboriginals became British subjects in 1948, but it wasn't until a year after I was born, 1967, that it was written into the constitution. Even so, many decades lapsed before Aboriginal people gained anything close to equality within the Australian community, and the health and economic gaps between Indigenous and non-Indigenous people seemed insurmountable in the late 1980s.

Added to that, my light skin made me worry that no one would ever take me seriously if I started identifying as a Blackfella. I was scared people would call me a fake or something equally as awful, so I trod carefully among both the white and Black communities as I came to terms with my Aboriginality. Becoming comfortable with my new identity would take some getting used to.

Claiming my identity made me feel more confident. At the time of the revelation I was still employed as a youth worker in the refuge for young women. When I shared my news with my co-workers they were totally shocked, not because I had announced I was Aboriginal but because they couldn't believe I had not known this myself. They had all understood I was Aboriginal but assumed I didn't make an issue of it, which was why I had never formally mentioned it. It seemed just because it had been a surprise to me didn't mean it was a surprise to anyone else – or really anyone else's business to determine.

Because of the Stolen Generations there were many Aboriginal people across Australia who did not know they had Aboriginal heritage. Thousands of children had been removed from their families and relocated into Aboriginal missions and adopted into white families. Those with lighter skin were often assumed to be white in greater society, and their lighter skin could sometimes act as protection against the racism and prejudice that was so commonly directed at darker-skinned Aboriginal people.

I was distanced from my Aboriginal heritage in ways that were profound yet understandable. Although not a member of the Stolen Generations I never felt truly connected with my maternal grandparents, and as a result I didn't understand that this secret was embedded in their history. A lot of healing needed to be done across Aboriginal communities that had been torn apart by years of institutional racism and abuse.

This is why I am such a strong voice for allowing Aboriginal people to self-determine whether they have Aboriginal heritage or Aboriginal identity. There is a distinct difference between these two terms that is often misunderstood. I only truly came to understand the difference more recently, and I started to see how the stages of understanding and acceptance of Aboriginal heritage were articulated through the process of ticking a box.

The first stage is when someone makes the choice to understand and accept their Aboriginal heritage. I started this step during my conversation with my mother on that day many years ago as she patiently explained that I was as much a part of her ancestry as I was of my father's. This stage usually leads to a person exploring and tracing their origins through an Aboriginal heritage passed on from within their family's bloodlines, which allows a person and those around them to first understand and acknowledge their Aboriginal ancestry and then value and develop a connection with that ancestry. Some people of Aboriginal descent choose to remain at this stage, while others continue on to embrace their Aboriginal identity.

This is the process of not just acknowledging their ancestry but making a choice to integrate aspects of the culture into their lives. Identity can be a hard thing to define, but in this case it is usually regarded as a person's qualities, beliefs and personality and their sense of self defined by physical, psychological and interpersonal characteristics that are shared with other persons within the same group. It also includes a range of affiliations, cultural responsibilities and cultural expectations.

Most people grow up immersed in their culture and connected with their families. However, due to the historical issues with Aboriginal child removal the self-protective mechanism of others not to openly identify as Aboriginal, along with the separation of Aboriginal people from their Country and a long-standing institutional attitude of whiteness being the more-important and most-dominant cultural aspect of Australian life, many people of Aboriginal heritage have not had the opportunity to directly engage with their immediate or extended family or have been distanced from the cultural aspects of their ancestry. For this reason, when we talk about Aboriginal self-identification we acknowledge this can occur directly or indirectly, from parents, friends or peers or other role models including elders or simply by the environment in which the person lives.

One thing I learned as I started my journey to cultural acceptance was that a person can have Aboriginal heritage without going through the process of self-defining themselves as having an Aboriginal identity. It doesn't make them less Aboriginal; it just suggests there are other factors at play that may make it uncomfortable, impractical or unnecessary to claim Aboriginal identity. Through the acknowledgement of Aboriginal heritage they can still come to value their heritage without being required to immerse themselves fully within Aboriginal culture, and for many coming to their identity later in life this can be an important first or final step in their decision to embrace their culture.

Even though I knew my Aboriginal family and lived much of my childhood on my Country, I had spent most of my years believing I was white. Thus, accepting my Aboriginal identity was not something I could do overnight, and particularly not as I had to fight resistance from both my husband's family and my paternal family.

Allen's family were very middle-class, hard-working people from regional New South Wales, living lives in towns where you would ride horses to school. These small towns often had long-held biases against the Blackfellas who populated the towns and areas around their homes.

Allen's family struggled to accept the fact that their granddaughters were Aboriginal and often found interesting ways to deny that reality. Allen's mum's favourite response when I reminded her that me and my children were Aboriginal would reply, 'Yes, but you're not a real one.'

I wasn't one for challenging my in-laws, and at first I ignored her when she said this. I also ignored it when she said to me that I was just trying to be Aboriginal. As years plodded along I found it harder and harder to let such comments slide and particularly when, as I was driving Teniel to her grandparents one day, she innocently piped up from her booster seat: 'Mum, when I get to Nan's please don't make me be Ab-bor-dig-inal.'

Tears sprang in my eyes. Children are attuned very early in life to understand whether or not they are accepted for who they are. At four years of age my daughter knew that to be accepted by her nan, whom she loved to death, she could not be Aboriginal. What kind of lesson is that for any child?

I knew I couldn't change my in-laws's attitude, but I could make damn sure that my children grew up knowing that me and their father fully accepted and loved them for all of who they were. Thankfully Allen was absolutely fine with the news that

I was embracing my heritage and never once made me feel less than because of my Aboriginality. As we continued to expand our family our children were all recognised as Aboriginal and he has supported this.

It was hard enough knowing that my husband's family struggled to accept who I was, but it was heartbreaking when I received pushback from my own family.

My father's sisters, parents, brothers and extended family had always been incredibly important to me. I cared what they thought of me, and the fact that they didn't immediately embrace my Aboriginality was more hurtful than I was able to articulate to them. I knew their response came not from prejudice but from their sense of hurt and rejection: they were not Aboriginal, and as far as they were concerned I was one of them and always had been. They didn't understand what they had done to make me reject them. We were close, so how could I want to reject who they were and declare myself something else entirely?

They asked my dad to intervene, to talk me out of this self-declaration of mine. He said 'No.' They were confused. Why was he okay with this? Wasn't it an even bigger rejection of him and his culture than it was of theirs? My dad didn't see it that way and refused to try to persuade me from my chosen course. Even my stepmother stood up for me in this, partly because it provided her with a great opportunity to gang up against my dad's family but mostly because, for Dad, Jackie and my step-sisters, Shannon and I being Aboriginal wasn't an issue at all.

As I started to explore what my identity really meant in 20th- and 21st-century Australia I often found them standing beside me willing to also fight for Black causes and challenge anyone who was derogatory towards Aboriginal people. I can even go as far as to say they were proud that I stood up and was counted as being Aboriginal. It was harder for the rest of my paternal family, though, and I remember going to a large family gathering at my Aunty Maureen's not long after I had begun to talk about my Aboriginal identity. Almost everyone from my father's family was there and it was a time of celebration and family togetherness, which I usually relished. However, in the middle of the festivities one of my cousins chose to publicly call me out.

'Why are you doing this to our family?' he asked, indicating my desire to call myself an Aboriginal.

My hands shook but I felt I had to defend myself. 'I am not doing anything to anyone. My mother is Aboriginal, her family is Aboriginal.'

My cousin just scoffed, hiding it behind a joking voice. 'You don't even look Aboriginal. You don't have skinny ankles,' he said, laughing.

This remark was so unexpected and incongruous I had no response, and I fled the party upset and crying. I thought that was the end, that I would never find a way to get back to the relationships I had always counted on with my aunties, nanna and cousins. However, perhaps because for the first time the rest of my family actually heard for themselves how awful and racist this attitude was they started to reconsider their positions. Whatever the reason, I felt a shift in attitudes the next time I shared time with members of my father's family, and after that incident I never had another family member challenge my choice to be Aboriginal. As the years passed and I achieved many things as an Aboriginal woman they became prouder of me and openly claimed me as their own, as I claim them as mine. I was still one of them; it just took them a little while to realise it.

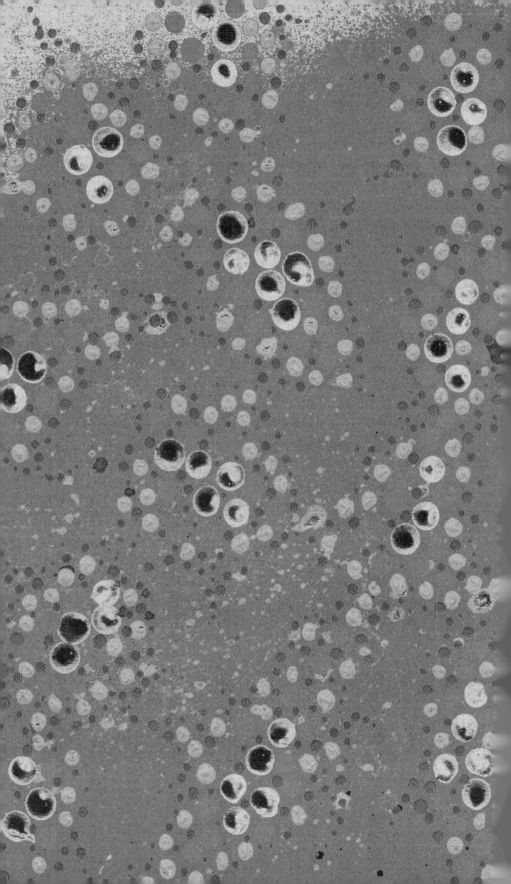

22. FINDING A MISSION

History repeats itself endlessly for those who are unwilling to learn from the past.

– LEON BROWN

Recognising my Aboriginality allowed me to understand more about myself and my mother's family. I also started to explore Aboriginal history and the difficulties Aboriginal communities face. As Aboriginal Peoples – or First Nations People as 'they' like us to call ourselves now – we are the survivors of genocide. Many people, including those living in this country, have no idea our ancestors survived intentional acts of genocide to eradicate a race of people. It sounds so very harsh to state it, but it is a shameful reality of this nation we humbly refer to as the 'lucky country'. Lucky for some!

Prior to the birth of my second child I found myself working in child protection. I had entered the system simply as a child protection caseworker because positions specific for Aboriginal caseworkers didn't exist, but as soon as I started gaining a reputation for myself I found the confidence to insist that the expertise of Aboriginal people working within the child protection system needed to be recognised and formalised. I began what became a five-year mission to establish Aboriginal-identified positions within the child welfare system as well as advocate for Aboriginal foster carers and workers.

This was needed because Aboriginal people have different needs within the welfare system, created in large part by the harmful and negative results of earlier so-called Aboriginal welfare legislation. The Aborigines Protection Act of 1909 was supposedly set up to help Aboriginal Australians overcome disadvantage by assimilating into white Australia, or where that was not possible be separated from it through a network of Aboriginal missions and townships.

This led directly to a policy of forced removal of Aboriginal children from their families. The act assumed that Aboriginal people were a dying race, and its objective was the forced assimilation of future generations. The chief protector had wide-reaching power as legal guardian of all Aboriginal children under the age of 16. And as a result the department he ran had the right to remove any Aboriginal child from their parents and place them into government- and church-run homes, where they were often adopted out to white people who required slave labour.

The effects of the Aborigines Protection Act were far from protective. It enabled the removal of anyone deemed to be an Aboriginal native or of mixed descent to a reserve, and any child under the age of 16 deemed to be an Aboriginal native to a state institution. Lighter-skinned children were more likely to be separated and placed in white homes, where they were raised without direct knowledge of and certainly no connection with their Aboriginal families or heritage. This is what is now call the Stolen Generations, and it continued as policy in different guises well into the 1980s.

There is little doubt that the ultimate intent of this policy was the destruction of Aboriginal society and culture, which were deemed to be savage and backward by the European powers that had invaded the country. The concept of savagery and primitive evolution was a concept of race theory that ranked different people based on their cultural development. The theory was based on Charles Darwin's proposition that through the process of evolution the brain began to increase in size and thus intelligence increased.

Aboriginal people and our cultures date back thousands of years and link us closely with some of the first people in the world and the Australian government, influenced by Darwinian theories, erroneously decided this meant we must have been the least intelligent race in the world and therefore incapable of looking after ourselves or, more importantly, our children.

Based on the information they were receiving from other governments and scientific communities of the time this may have seemed like a reasonable and even well-intentioned idea by those who supported it, and unsurprisingly many white people honestly believed that these poor black children truly needed white people's help to master basic life skills or else they would live lives of utter misery in primitive conditions. The fact that these life skills seemed to be taught mostly through the practice of forcing Aboriginal children to work for white people, mainly cooking, cleaning and labouring on farms and stations, was never really questioned as closely as it should have been then.

I want to make it clear I am not blaming anyone today for the actions undertaken against Aboriginal people in the past. I do not believe there is any benefit in engaging in accusations or the shaming of people for things they personally did not have any hand in, and I do believe many who were involved may have had genuinely good intentions. This doesn't change the fact, though, that for Aboriginal people the past was traumatic and real harm was done. We have lived through invasion and oppression and are left with the legacy of invasion and transgenerational trauma and, for many of us, survivor's guilt.

As a community, and particularly as welfare workers and policy-makers more generally, we have to ensure that current and future policies do not cause more harm than good regardless of their good intentions. Despite the wealth and relative development of Australia as a nation over the past 200 years, Aboriginal people continue to be some of the most disadvantaged and we need to have policies and services to help rectify this.

It's important to acknowledge that although Aboriginal people make up only around 3.8 per cent of the Australian population (984,000 people in 2021), 85 per cent of child deaths in Australia are Aboriginal children and the average life expectancy of an Aboriginal person is considerably lower than the national average. I am one of only 11 per cent of Aboriginal people alive at my age, and in six years' time my age will reduce my percentage of life expectancy to 3 per cent.

Knowing this history, people ask me why I would want to work in an area that is characterised by the removal of children from families. I reply that child protection is so much more than that, and it is important that Aboriginal people are active within the sector otherwise there is a complete lack of understanding of this history and how it may affect current and future generations of parents and children. While it can seem easy to look at child protection or interventionist policies as no more than modern-day versions of the Stolen Generations, and it is understandable that Aboriginal communities carrying trauma from the effects of forced removals are suspicious of child protection policies, the fact is that many Aboriginal children are definitely in need of protection and hard decisions have to be made in the child's best interest.

This does not mean, however, that we should allow child welfare agencies to remove or respond to Aboriginal children without taking into consideration the historical impacts of previous protection policies. Indeed, they should be even more mindful of these when engaging with Aboriginal children and their families. This is why I have worked so hard to create effective policies, guidelines and training throughout the child welfare section in relation to Aboriginal child protection, and why I have dedicated so much of my life to working with these agencies to ensure that when a child is removed it is only done as a last resort and with appropriate cultural and kinship placements.

I can understand the concerns, but what the community doesn't often see is the number of times Aboriginal child protection workers like me are able to intervene and prevent children from being removed by recommending other actions be taken prior to removal being considered. I cannot tell you how many times I have prevented Aboriginal children from being taken into care but, because of our commitment to confidentiality, it is often difficult to get these stories out there and the stubborn stain of previous generational trauma continues to make modern child protection a difficult and complicated procedure. Sometimes it feels that Aboriginal child protection workers are often damned if they work for the welfare system and damned if they don't.

I believe I have made a difference, but even today I know that although sometimes it is absolutely essential that an Aboriginal child be removed from a situation that is neglectful or abusive, not all Aboriginal kids in care should be in care. Sometimes our kids are taken from their homes or communities when other, more effective options are available, and sometimes they shouldn't be part of child protective orders at all.

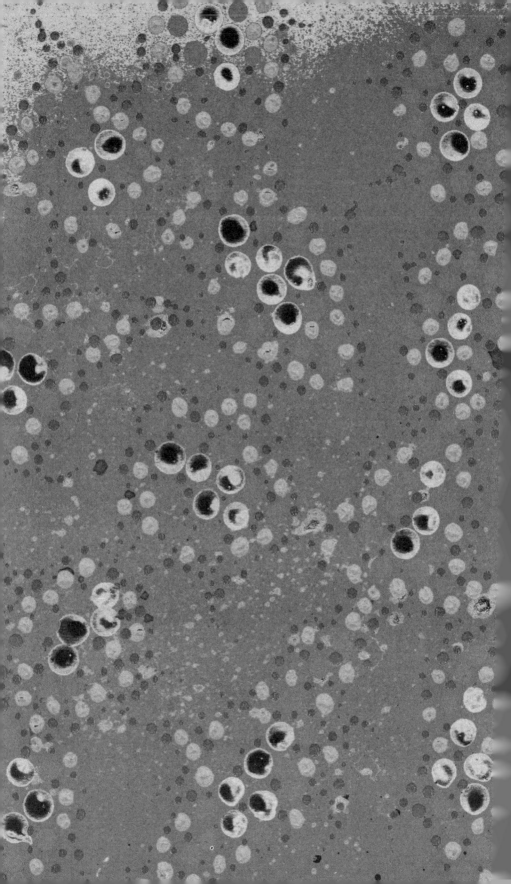

23. CHILD PROTECTION WORKER

Even if you're on the right track, you'll
get run over if you just sit there.

– WILL ROGERS

Working in child protection could be dangerous at times. Many of us worked under aliases such as maiden names so we could prevent being easily found by aggrieved parents or family members. My maiden name was Brown, which was a real godsend as it made it next to impossible to identify and find me back in the days when we still relied on a phone book to track people down. Despite my desire to take Allen's surname and have a united family once Teniel was born, I was still using my maiden name professionally and it seemed easier not to go through all the rigmarole of officially changing all the documentation. Ironically, in the end I ended up having a different surname from my children after all.

At times I did think about adopting my husband's name officially, if only to give our family that sense of unity, but as it turned out my decision not to do so ended up being the thing that possibly saved my family's life.

I had been working on a particularly difficult case involving an HIV-positive father who was imprisoned for the sexual assault of young children and babies. Each month I accompanied his three-year-old daughter to the jail for a supervised parental visit. I always found these visits extremely uncomfortable, as the child was too young to really converse with her father and the man would often use these visits to engage in conversation with me, usually concerning what his life was going to be like when he was released from prison and how he intended to live in an imagined happy family with his child.

I knew this was not going to be a possibility and usually tried to change the subject or ignore his demands, scooping up the child

115

with a relieved sigh as soon as the designated half-hour visitation had elapsed. However, on one particular visit the man was more demanding than usual and I realised that the end of his prison term was in sight. I felt it was important for him to understand that there was no scenario where his daughter would be returned to his unsupervised care.

'Why not?' he demanded.

'Because you have been convicted on child sexual assault charges,' I explained patiently. 'The department cannot allow you access to any children upon your release, even your own child. You will get visitation, supervised, but that is all you can hope for.' I sat back as the man's eyes turned cold and grey with anger and resentment.

'That's bloody bullshit,' he said. 'I wouldn't touch my own daughter. That's disgusting.'

I blinked and shook my head, but he understood from what I wasn't saying: *'Mate, you have to be kidding!'*

The man just shrugged and in a chilling tone responded. 'Yeah, well, it's not my fault parents don't look after their children properly. They shouldn't leave them with me.'

Having worked with perpetrators for long enough by then I understood there was a very real chance he would never harm his own child and that he really believed in what he was saying. He equally believed it was the parents' fault for entrusting the care of their children to him. This man raped babies, yet he felt we should hand over his baby to him in the certainty he wouldn't subject her to the same fate as other children! I met some despicable parents in my time, but he was one of the worst.

Given this man was due for release the following year, I reported this information to the police and we set about getting court orders to prevent him from ever having unsupervised contact with his daughter again. I was successful in my court application, but it gave me no pleasure knowing his little girl would not understand why she couldn't live with her daddy. I wished things had been different, not only for his daughter but for the other children he raped.

He found out about the court orders a few months before his release, and on our next custody visit he was incensed and screamed at me that I would not keep his child from him. I was thankful the prison guards intervened so quickly, but not before he threatened both me and my family if his daughter was not returned to him once he left prison. I was shaken and it was determined that prison visitations would be suspended. A new caseworker and police protection were to be organised for his supervised visits with the child once he was released.

I thought that was the end of the matter and tried to push him out of my mind, but it was not easy. It wasn't that he had threatened my family and me, because I had been threatened many times before; it was that this man felt so entitled to his child despite all the harm and trauma he had caused. He had no concept of his own evil, and those people are the ones who never truly reform. I knew any child unlucky enough to end up in his unsupervised presence would be extremely vulnerable. At least I had helped ensure that his child was safe.

Upon his release the man unsuccessfully tried to overturn the visitation decision and his wrath turned on me. He did everything he could to track me down, leaving messages at my workplace and telling anyone he encountered that he was going to find my children and rape them, thus giving them HIV. He never did find us, mainly because of the precautions I had taken to keep my family separate from my work and the use of my maiden name, but this whole episode proved how important some aspects of anonymity are when you work in the area of child protection.

Not that it was always the parents who caused the problems.

On one occasion we became involved with a family after the father had suddenly passed away in bizarre circumstances: his four-year-old son accidentally stabbed him in the leg with a lead pencil and he got blood poisoning and died shortly after. The children's mum had left years ago and had no interest in resuming care of the boy and his siblings, so we had to find a suitable foster family to care for them.

We found some distant family in another state in the place where the father had been born, and set about arranging for them to take on the care of the children. Simultaneously, we arranged for the father's body to be transported for burial within this same community, because it is incredibly important that family be together on their Country.

The word 'Country' in Aboriginal terms means a particular geographical area. Aboriginal Countries are similar to what whitefellas would call regions or districts. In Aboriginal Australia we have approximately 253 Countries that are recognised and accepted by the Australian government. Each Country can be compared with countries in Europe as each has its own language, belief system, values, traditions and ceremonies; the people can also often look different. Prior to invasion and then colonisation, Blackfellas did not cross into each other's Country without permission. Our Elders ensured there was no inter-breeding among our people and often arranged marriages to benefit the different communities, so some families can have a few ancestral Countries. If a mob needed a person with specific skills such as a hunter or weaver then the matches would be made to ensure the mob's survival.

As we began the task of returning the five children to their Country we were advised that the children's behaviour was challenging and that transporting them would probably require three child protection workers to suitably supervise all of them. It was the four year old who obviously needed the most supervision, as his behaviour issues were clear and evident from the beginning.

On the very first day as we changed planes for the second leg of our journey heading towards a remote coastal Aboriginal community this child wandered away from us and up to a pair of police officers in Melbourne airport, then confidently asked if he could have one of their guns so he could shoot some people. The officers looked concerned and I took charge of the boy, hastily leading him away and explaining to the officers that I was not the child's mother but a child protection worker supervising the child. I assured them that the child was not being serious, although even now I'm not sure if that was true or not.

The rest of the journey was equally fraught, except instead of just one challenging child we had five of them – and we had them for more than four days. The kids spent almost the entire journey literally beating the crap out of each other: no-holds-barred, violent, sustained aggression that took all three caseworkers to break up. As soon as we got one fight under control another broke out and we had to prise the children apart, unclenching fists from hair and holding back limbs that were flailing in violent punches and kicks.

We finally arrived at the first stop of the journey, the home of one of the children's uncles who had agreed to look after the children for the night to break up our trip. It was late afternoon when we arrived at the house and, exhausted from our travels, I sat in the living room with one of the other caseworkers and briefed the man and his wife about the children's situation while the other caseworker did a quick look around the bedrooms for a final check. Throughout our conversation there was a persistent thud, thud, thud coming from the front yard. It sounded like the kids were bouncing a ball against the wall and none of us paid much attention to the gentle sounds.

Upon completing the handover and with some sense of relief that the kids were not our responsibility for at least one night, we walked outside to say our goodbyes. Our freedom from the children was just steps away when the conversation turned deadly quiet. I turned to look at what everyone else was already looking at, and I swear there wasn't a brick on the front of the uncle and aunt's home that wasn't splattered with mud. In total disbelief and seeing our freedom slip away before our eyes I spluttered out an apology, wondering how the hell we would get the mud off the front of the house.

The uncle just smiled at me, then gently pointed me and the other workers towards the direction of our vehicle and said with a sly smile on his face, 'This is where you walk away and we deal with this the Blackfella way, the way uncles do it.' No one asked what that actually meant, because ignorance at that time was our ticket to the freedom of a motel room, meal and bed to finally unwind from our extraordinarily stressful day. I think we were all afraid that if we asked too many questions the aunt and uncle might change their mind and send the children back with us.

The following day we bravely returned to begin the four-hour drive to reunite the children with the rest of their family and prepare them for their dad's funeral later that day. When we arrived the front of the home had been cleaned of any evidence of the onslaught it had copped the day before, and the aunt and uncle assured us with grins on their faces that the children had had a good night. As the children piled into our van they were unusually quiet and obedient. I don't know exactly what the uncle's way of doing things was but I couldn't see any evidence of bruising or marks. Whatever it had been, it seemed to do the trick without injury.

As we drove in relative peace we felt confident enough to stop for lunch and let the kids play for a short while in a park. The park had a small playground area with a large domed structure that kids could clamber about on. The kids made a beeline for it but only the eldest was able to navigate his way to the top. He stood above his siblings boasting and crowing as the other children tried and failed to get up to him. Frustrated, one of the smaller children picked up a stone and threw it up at the eldest boy. It missed him by a mile, but it sparked an idea and soon the other kids were pelting rocks and stones and pebbles up at the boy.

He was high enough to escape most of them, although more than one or two hit their mark. He had a difficult choice to make: stay on the top of the structure, where most of the projectiles could not reach him but where he would be trapped, or try to get down and therefore within range of the rocks being thrown at him.

To say I disliked the eldest child was an understatement. He was downright mean and had absolutely no respect for anyone, so when he was being pelted with rocks and screaming at us to help him selective deafness overcame me. Apparently this anomaly was going around that day, because none of us heard him yelling for help or went to his aid. It became a bit of a stalemate, as the children on the ground were relentless and didn't stop throwing rocks until they finally got tired out. At that time the eldest child scampered down and another fight broke out. We stopped that one, as we needed to head off and get the kids delivered in time for their father's funeral.

The small community church where the funeral was being held was so full when we arrived that half the guests had to stand outside. We stood with them listening to the service, which was amplified through a fuzzy microphone. Most of the children were inside with their family, although one of the younger children emerged as we arrived and came over to stand next to me, taking my hand as the eulogies for her father were read and recited.

As I stood there outside the church with the girl's grubby, soft hand in mine I started to feel the tension and stress of the journey ebb away, and for the first time I began to feel real sympathy for these little children. They may have been badly behaved and uncontrollable, but they were children who had lost both their parents and were now trying to find their way in a place filled with strangers. For this little girl I was probably one of the most familiar people she knew.

I reached down and stroked her head. Something moved under my fingertips and I looked down, realising with horror that there was a large colony of lice climbing through her hair and on her clothes. There were more lice than I had ever seen in my entire life, let alone on one head. My head started itching the moment I caught sight of those disgusting bugs.

I discreetly motioned to the other two workers to alert them to the crawling head, and as the other children came within our reach we quickly established that all five children were teaming with nits. We had been in close contact with the children for the past two days, and within moments we began subtly scratching our heads under the guise of fixing and straightening our hairstyles. I desperately longed to get away from there and back to the hotel where I could treat my hair, but there was still a way to go with the service and we couldn't leave.

The children were buzzing around us and it was difficult to keep a distance from them, although I tried not to get too close. The funeral director came over to us and advised that they would be closing the coffin soon, so if the children wanted to say their goodbyes it had to be done straight away. A couple of the children expressed their desire to see their dad for the last time, so I escorted them into the church to say their final goodbyes.

Let me set the scene. We had a father who had sadly passed away due to blood poisoning from being stabbed in the leg with a lead pencil by one of his children. We had a community in mourning for the loss of their loved one. We had family members who were now welcoming five orphaned children back into their care and reuniting them with their community. This was a sad day, and all eyes were on the poor children and the welfare workers who had brought the children home.

We weren't exactly the enemy on this occasion as we were returning the children to their families and Country but, still, many of the people sitting in that church had their own stories of being stolen or removed by so-called do-gooders. I was very aware that I was being watched with suspicion and dislike as I walked the children to the coffin to say their goodbyes to their dad. As I stood there with the six year old everyone in that whole church laser focused on us. He stopped just short of the coffin, looked up to me and yelled at the top of his voice, 'He stinks! Can't you smell him? He really stinks!' If the ground had opened up and swallowed me I would have been nothing but grateful. Thankfully, as we left the church most of the eyes tracking us were either full of sympathy towards the child or trying really hard not to laugh out loud.

After the funeral the three of us workers drove the four hours back to the city, all madly scratching our heads the entire way. As soon as we arrived in town we hunted for a late-night chemist and bought their three remaining bottles of nit solution.

24. TALES FROM THE FRONTLINE

[E]veryone's drowning at work, but [we're] all so used to it.

– JODIE SHAW

Life as a child protection officer was often difficult and challenging, and I have to admit that I made my fair share of mistakes. I sometimes got compassion fatigue or depressed by the bureaucracy. I was on a steep learning curve as I learned the ropes and navigated a system that can be frustrating and tiresome and sometimes downright impossible. However, with the support of mentors and an understanding of the importance of the work I was doing I began to build a reputation within the organisation as a dedicated and capable caseworker. More importantly, my local Aboriginal community started to trust and respect me as someone who could be relied upon to at least ensure Aboriginal voices were at the table.

Over time it was common for a variety of organisations to contact me directly when they had concerns for an Aboriginal family, and I was often able to work with these families before the issues became child protection concerns.

Despite the hardships and lack of resources I loved my work as a child protection officer and later as a manager, and I was excited to have the chance to focus on the needs of Aboriginal parents, communities and children. In child protection you meet all types of families: those that are just having a tough time and with some support can get back on track, and others that are not able to do enough to ensure their children's safety. These situations can be particularly difficult when the family is Aboriginal.

Although they'd had a great deal of support, one family who had been in the system for many years were not providing what was necessary for their child's welfare. The problem was that no one else in the department had the courage to intervene with this family for fear of being called racist. The welfare agencies wanted to do the right thing, but this was often not clear cut when working with Aboriginal families.

The history of the Stolen Generations and the forced removal of children from Aboriginal communities had had long and terrible consequences for both Aboriginal peoples and those in the communities who were genuinely trying to do their best for Aboriginal children. No one trusted anyone else, so sometimes families were kept together when they shouldn't be or split up when other options were available. Not having enough Aboriginal people working within the system added to the difficulties, as the underlying issues were often left unaddressed and Aboriginal communities often saw any intervention as the white system once again interfering and breaking up their families.

In this particular case the children were at significant risk and something had to be done. It became one of my first really trying cases as an Aboriginal child protection worker, and although I was able to address many of the more general concerns the distrust and suspicion of the Aboriginal community and their advocates led to this case turning into more of a fight than it should ever have been. Eventually, after a six-month battle the children's court finally granted me permission to remove the children from their parents' care.

This was in no small part because of my commitment to ensuring they were placed in a culturally appropriate placement where the family's community would be involved in consultation and ongoing communication as the family was supported to turn the situation around. I wasn't sure the family would be in a position to do so, though, as the children had been exposed to some horrific abuse during their lives including severe neglect, physical injuries and sexual abuse from a relative. Their treatment had been a direct result of their parents' inability to provide safety and supervision for them.

Extensive planning took place to ensure the removal occurred with the least amount of trauma to the children. After an extremely difficult and stressful few days of planning, including arranging police protection for us, we finally had the children in our care and were heading to the foster care placement. When we arrived at the address

I hustled the kids out of the car and up the driveway to the front door. I knocked on the door, and it was promptly answered by a lovely gentleman who looked of Indian descent. This was a little surprising, as I had worked hard to ensure the children were placed with Aboriginal foster carers. One of my main initiatives since establishing an Aboriginal child protection department within the child protection office had been to ensure we were able to place any removed children into a culturally appropriate Aboriginal family.

It had been a long and stressful day and so, trusting that all due diligence had been done by the placement team, I assumed that perhaps this man or his partner were Aboriginal. After all, with my lighter skin I was hardly anyone to judge who was or was not Aboriginal based purely on appearance.

One thing that really concerns me is that Aboriginal people are often judged by the colour of their skin. Nowhere is there anything that says Aboriginality is determined by the depth of skin colour, but somehow there are some Aboriginal and whitefellas who use this as a way to have power over other Aboriginal fellas with lighter skin. It's always been an issue close to my heart because I've copped my fair share of racism due to the light colour of my skin, by both Blackfellas and whitefellas. It's not my fault I have light skin! My skin colour is a result of invasion more than 200 years ago, which is something I had no control over.

I pulled out the paperwork and started the official handover of the children. The man seemed somewhat flustered, but I assumed this was because we had been a little late getting the children to the address than we had advised the foster carers. This also explained why the man's wife was not there awaiting our arrival: she had, the man explained when I asked about her whereabouts, gone down to the shops to get some groceries but would be home shortly.

The children quickly ducked in front of me and went inside and started playing with other children in the house. The man said nothing, just looked at the children for a long moment, then he turned back to me and listened politely as I explained the details of the children's care. After making sure he had all the details I said my goodbyes to the children, who were still busy playing with the other kids, and walked out the door, telling the man I would call tomorrow to see how the children had settled in. When I was halfway down the drive the man called out in a somewhat alarmed tone.

'Sorry, are you leaving these children here?'

I turn back, confused. 'Yes,' I replied, a bit irritated.

'I'm sorry: I don't know who you are or why these children are here?'

In that split second 100 things went through my mind. Foremost was annoyance: I simply didn't have time for this. Where the hell was his wife anyway, and why would she go out when she must have been expecting our visit? Why didn't she tell her husband what was happening? Then it dawned on me that maybe there really had been some kind of mistake.

'You are the Aboriginal foster carer, aren't you?'

The man shook his head. 'No.'

I quickly scanned the paperwork I held in my hand, hoping that this was just a case of a rather absent-minded man who had not been paying attention as his wife made all the arrangements, but as I read the address on the form I realised my mistake. Canberra likes to reuse a lot of street names, so the trick is you have to ensure you have the correct suburb. In this case I was several suburbs away from where I needed to be. Red faced and apologising profusely, I rushed back into the house and prised the children from the game they were playing with their newfound friends and quickly got them back into the car, hoping like hell this man wouldn't remember my name or call my boss to complain!

Over the following years I often wondered what would have happened had I actually left the children there. How would the man have explained it to his wife upon her return: 'Look, honey, a strange lady dropped off some more children for us!'

During these crazy times Allen and I welcomed our second daughter Cassie-lee into the world. My sister Shannon had come from Queensland for the pending birth, and I dutifully went into labour in August 1994.

During Teniel's labour I had requested an epidural because, I'm not ashamed to say, I am not a fan of pain, but the medical staff had told me my labour was too far advanced and I had to give birth without pain relief. This time I was prepared: I made sure I convinced the doctors as early in the labour as possible that the pain was simply unbearable and that I wanted to get to the hospital well before midnight even if I wasn't quite ready to be admitted. You see, I had learned the hard way that the anaesthetist at the hospital went off duty at midnight, so if you came in after that your chances of getting the proper good stuff for pain relief was basically zilch.

Suitably medicated, I began the real business of labour in the early hours of the morning and by midday our little girl had been born, mum and baby safe and healthy after a relatively painless birth! Cassie-lee weighed just over 3 kilograms and was beautiful in every way possible.

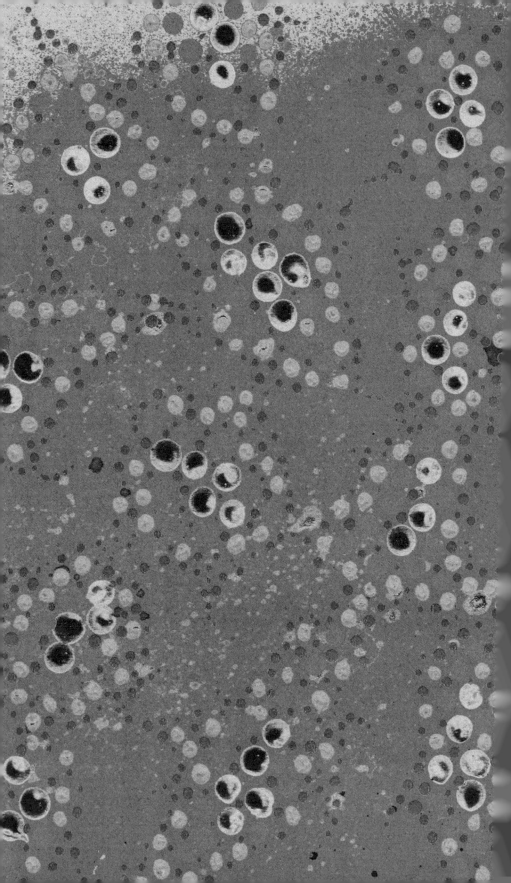

25. REMEMBERING CATHY

You know nothing, Jon Snow.

– YGRITTE, *GAME OF THRONES*

When I decided to work in the child protection area I knew there would be times when my values would be challenged, and that keeping my mouth shut would be even more challenging. In this job we worked with families and children who have had awful things happen to them, and I have always said that just sheer luck and a supportive family have been the difference between me and some of the families I work with. At the time child protection services were reactive, and I normally only dealt with families once they had reached the threshold of serious concerns for children's safety. It is very different from today, where best practice includes early intervention systems to prevent families from coming into the child protection system.

In 1998 I was told to attend the hospital as a mother had tried to take the life of herself and her three-year-old child. Mum had purposefully walked out on a highway holding her child with the intent of being hit by the next car that came along. That next vehicle was a van driven by a bloke innocently driving to work sitting on the 100 kilometre per hour speed limit, and the rest you can guess.

Before going to the hospital I spoke with the police officer who had attended the accident. He cried, telling me that he had been on the job for a long time and had never experienced anything like that before. He had just left the smash repair shop where the van had been towed, and he described the driver as being so traumatised he was unable to be interviewed.

Both mother and child survived the impact; however, the child's injuries were worse than the mother's. Most of the bones in the three year old's body had been broken, and while Mum had a few broken bones she was mobile enough to get around in a wheelchair. I remembered driving to the hospital with a co-worker thinking to myself: 'Fuck you, mother, you're not getting your daughter back.'

After arriving at the hospital we went to the toddler's room and I pulled up short at the door, shocked by how much plaster covered the little girl. Sitting beside her was her dad, who was understandably upset at seeing his daughter like that. I made it to the end of her bed, then had to turn around and walk out. There's not much I can't handle, but this was too much. I had given birth to my third child, Jenna, in 1998 in that very same hospital, and she was so loved. As I stood in that hospital room for those few moments before fleeing my head was flooded by visions of someone doing this to any of my girls. How could a mother do this to their child? I wouldn't think twice if I was in a position where I had to kill to protect my children, but that's where my deadly thoughts would end.

Thank god my co-worker and I had worked together for many years, so when she saw me leave the room she seamlessly took over as if nothing had happened. I went in search of the mum and found her in her hospital room. I began the interview with such calmness that no one would have known what was going through my head or how my soul hurt at the thought of having to even speak to the woman. I was in no doubt that what this woman had done was pure evil, and I knew as I walked into her room that she would pay for what she had done. At the very least she would never be able to hurt her poor child again, assuming the girl survived the injuries this woman had inflicted on her.

Just when you think you know everything the universe has a special way of kicking your legs out from under you and putting you on your arse. I had worked in child protection for many years by then and had heard and seen many things the average person would have nightmares about, but there was a phenomenon for situations such as this that had a flash term for it: vicarious trauma.

Vicarious trauma is the emotional residue collected by caseworkers and others who work in traumatic and emotionally damaging workplaces. It is the effect of being exposed to victims and perpetrators as they talk about and relive their trauma stories: the listener not only witnesses the pain, fear and terror that trauma survivors have endured and sometimes empathises with it, but they often internalise that pain as a result of having to carry it vicariously.

This type of trauma most often manifests in the form of burnout, depression, nightmares and stress. The story I was about to hear from this young mother was one of the most traumatic I had ever encountered, perhaps because I had gone into that interview so sure I knew what the story was and who was to blame. What she told me left me with nightmares for years afterwards.

This mother loved her daughter: truly, deeply, completely. I would have argued with anyone who tried to tell me that, knowing as I did that this same mother had just tried to kill her child on the highway, but it was true. She had not gone onto the highway in order to kill her child, but rather to try and save them both. At first I couldn't understand what she was saying, how this could ever be considered an act of kindness.

'Because it was the only way out,' she told me.

She went on to describe the life she had been living, a life of severe emotional and psychological abuse as she was controlled and dominated by a cruel and manipulative man who imprisoned her in their home. He withheld or poisoned her food and cut off contact with anyone outside the house, keeping her a virtual prisoner as he starved and tormented her. He threatened to kill the child if the mother tried to escape and she honestly believed he would do so, but she also knew that the years of abuse were catching up with her. She was weak and sickly, unable to do much of anything in her fragile condition.

'I knew it was just a matter of time,' she whispered, 'before he finally did it. I was so sick all the time, so weak. And when I died I knew, I knew he would start doing the same thing to her. I couldn't let that happen. I couldn't let him torture her for years the way he did to me.' My stomach was churning with horror. This man whom I had just glimpsed sitting so attentively at his injured child's bedside was some kind of monster. Could it be true?

The woman said that he had never harmed their child or kept food from her, but she was convinced that once she was gone his controlling ways would find a new target in their child. I believed the woman's story, because it was too detailed and her physical and emotional state too consistent with the tale she was telling for it to be anything but believable. However, that also meant she was telling the truth when she said the man had never harmed the child, while she had tried to kill both herself and her daughter. Placing the child back into her care was not possible, but I also had to make sure that the father didn't get sole custody – at least not until we could determine whether he posed any threat to his daughter.

The best I could do was to place the three year old in the care of her aunt. The father was allowed to move in with the aunt to co-parent, on the condition he was never to be alone or unsupervised with his daughter. The aunt lived interstate, so the case was transferred to other caseworkers and I was unable to find out what happened to the little girl after that. I still think about that case and hope that the close call of losing his daughter was the wake-up call the man needed to change his controlling ways, and that the mother got the help and support she needed.

I wasn't always unable to see the results of our interventions. Often I could work through a case right to the end, and these were often the most rewarding times during my years in child protection and youth and women's services.

One such case involved Julie, a mother aged around 30 whose child had been removed by another team after they had received reports that Julie was in a particularly vulnerable mental state. I am always concerned when services remove children, particularly young ones, from mothers who are struggling, as their situation is often the result of domestic violence issues and post-traumatic stress disorder (PTSD). In my experience, removing a child is rarely the best approach if the mother has already made steps to leave the relationship and deal with her trauma.

That was the case with Julie, who had left a particularly violent relationship a few months previously and found herself unable to fully cope with either her sole parental responsibilities or her mental state. She was struggling, but removing her child was not in my opinion the best way to help her through this difficult time in her life. Women need support and practical services to assist them to make the transition into a new, violence-free situation, not bureaucratic caseworkers making arbitrary decisions.

Upon hearing about her case I resolved to go and speak to Julie, and found her to be somewhat manic but coherent. I was frustrated that child removal had been so quickly agreed upon. Julie was not a threat to her child, and although she was certainly experiencing anxiety, depression and PTSD her mental state was being further impacted by the distress of having her two-year-old daughter taken into care. Unsurprisingly, she was suspicious and angry when I went to visit her and resistant to listening to me or trying to work with me to find a way to give both her and her daughter a more stable and supported environment. I couldn't really blame her: she had gone through hell, and as someone who has experienced my own fair share of crazy, emotional moments I could relate.

I also knew that until she got her health under control it was going to be difficult to reunite her with her child since the removal order had been enforced. I had to make her trust me and accept the help I was offering. It took some doing, but after a few days Julie began to give me the benefit of the doubt and we enrolled her in counselling and support services. I worked with the Department of Housing to find an apartment where she could safely raise her child.

I also convinced the department that Julie was perfectly fine to have extended and unsupervised visitations with her child throughout her recovery, because I knew that her connection with her daughter Chloe and the love she had for that child, a love that had finally motivated her to find the courage to leave an abusive long-term relationship, was the key ingredient in Julie's path to mental health and resilience.

We were also fortunate that the foster parents who were looking after Chloe were fully supportive of Julie's visitation and did everything they could to make it seem to Chloe that she was on a kind of holiday, rather than having been removed from her mother's care indefinitely. Foster carers like those involved in Julie and Chloe's case are the backbone of a strong and effective child protection system, and without them the outcomes for the children would be far more traumatic. It is true there are foster parents who are not in the system for the right reasons and some who, quite frankly, I wouldn't want looking after my pets never mind having the unsupervised care of children, but the majority of those who agree to be foster carers are amazing, unsung heroes. They rarely get the credit or respect they deserve for their tireless and selfless dedication to the welfare of the children in their care.

With hard work and Julie's dedication we were able to reunite mother and daughter just six months after the removal orders had been enforced, and Chloe was released into a stable and loving home with her mother. It was something that had seemed impossible to Julie when she first engaged with child protection authorities.

The thing I learned from this case was how important it was to support and consider the parent's mental health and practical needs. Child protection works when it is part of an integrated system that can help to link up parents with other services such as mental health care, housing, job training, child care and any other number of practical services that can be a huge struggle for those battling difficult circumstances. I have used the lessons I learned from Julie's case to help me ensure I made the very best decisions for both parent and child in my child protection role.

As a youth and child protection worker I had not got the opportunity to see the families whom I had worked with over the years; however, I often thought about them, about how they were doing and whether they had found happiness in their later lives.

It was a delightful surprise to come across Cathy, a young woman whom I had met while working in the youth refuge. I ran into her quite unexpectedly at a shopping centre in Canberra and recognised her instantly, even though she had aged a few years and was no longer the small, slim, timid girl I had known during her time there. She still had a shyness about her and continued to hide behind her long fringe, peering up with big brown eyes through her hair. She was pushing a small pram and had that happy but exhausted look that is almost uniform for all new mothers. I knew it well, as my first-born daughter Teniel had only come into the world a few months before this meeting.

'Melinda,' Cathy said nervously, recognising me as easily as I had recognised her. I asked her how she was going. 'I'm really good. I am so glad to see you.' Her voice was still low, almost a whisper, and I had to really listen to hear her. However, her words were happy and excited and not shaky or scared, the way she had seemed at the refuge.

'I'm really pleased to see you,' I responded, and then noticed the sleeping baby in the pram beside her. Cathy beamed at the infant. 'She's so little,' I said, smiling at the delicate features of the baby as she slept.

Cathy smiled. 'I gave birth a little over three months ago.'

'She is beautiful,' I said. 'I have a little one too. She's about the same age; her name is Teniel.' I pointed to my pram, where my black-haired baby was quietly sleeping.

'She's gorgeous,' Cathy said, 'and it's a great name.'

'What is your little one called?' I asked.

'Her name is Melinda,' Cathy said softly. 'I named her after you.'

I looked up, surprised, not sure I had understood what she had said. 'You did?' I asked.

Cathy nodded. 'I remember what you did for me, Melinda. I don't think I would be here without you, and my baby wouldn't be here either.'

Tears came to my eyes. How amazing it was to have had such an impact on people. I had known Cathy for only a few months after she had come to the refuge for protection from her father, who had been sexually abusing her for most of her life. I had not seen her for years, yet she had remembered me so fondly she named her baby after me. I think this is one thing we often don't realise: how much of an effect we have on other people and how important our connections may be, even if they only last a little while.

Sometimes when I wonder if I did any good at all in the world I remember Cathy and Julie and others like them. Even though I was awarded an ACT public service award for most improved services for Aboriginal and Torres Strait Islander families and young people, it is knowing I had some small part in improving the lives of people like Cathy that reminds me, despite all the difficulties, it was all worth it. As for awards: well, it's nice to win them, I guess, but honestly I didn't even go to the awards ceremony. There was a Blackfella child protection conference happening in Sydney at the same time and I wasn't going to miss that!

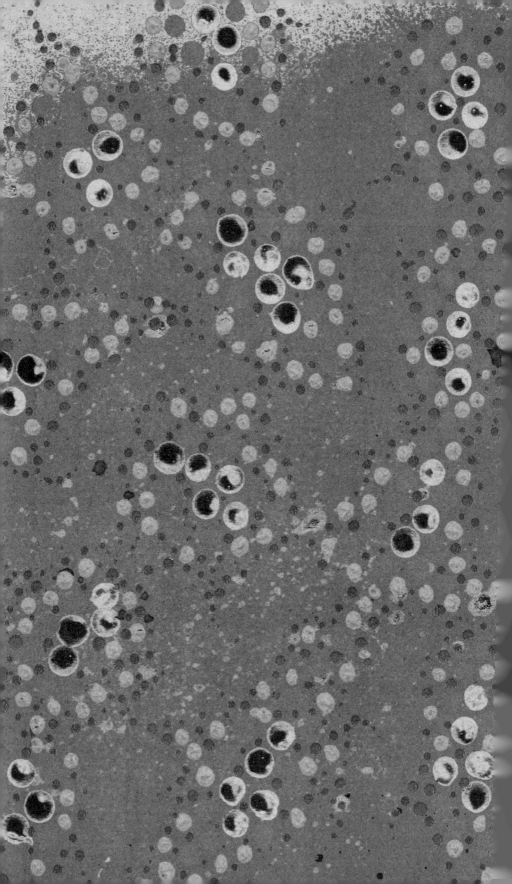

26. 'NOT EVEN ABORIGINAL'

In the event of a tornado or other such
natural disasters, place the wieners
and/or cheese slices in your pockets so
the search dogs will find you first.

– Unknown

Most people think that child welfare is all about going into people's homes and working with parents and children one on one, and there is a lot of that, but the role itself was surprisingly varied. One of the more unusual and interesting parts of my job was working as part of a disaster management team. Nowadays there is a more politically correct term for this part of the job. I think the current one is community recovery team, but I have always felt disaster was a more appropriate name for the experiences and situations we had to deal with both in and out of the office.

The disaster management team was all about preparing for and responding to the very worst-case scenarios, and it involved a lot of training in simulated disasters and crisis situations where child protection was a concern.

I remember one of the earlier training sessions was a simulated air crash at Canberra Airport. The actors were made up to look as though they had survived a horrific plane crash, blood and all, including some with debris from the plane protruding from parts of their bodies. It was frighteningly realistic. It was my job to triage the walking wounded, collect details for registering the injured and provide any initial crisis counselling they may require.

In my enthusiasm to help as many people as I could I may have inadvertently created a simulated zombie apocalypse, because even though the actors who were supposed to be dead had huge signs hanging from their necks that said 'Deceased' I was so focused on being diligent that I made them get up and give me all their details. I even gave a number of them what was, to be fair, fairly good crisis counselling that would have helped them a lot if they hadn't already been declared dead. Still, despite this small oversight I learned a huge amount in these simulations and found them surprisingly enjoyable, which probably wasn't the point of the exercise.

The skills I learned in those situations seemed a bit extreme at the time, but as it turned out they proved very necessary only a short time later.

The Royal Canberra Hospital demolition was, bizarrely, advertised as a wonderful day out for local Canberrans, so on 13 July 1997 thousands of families lined the banks of Lake Burley Griffin waiting to witness the planned implosion of one of Canberra's most iconic buildings. The local radio station ran a competition where the winner would be lucky enough to press the detonation button. It was all seen as a bit of fun, an opportunity to witness something that was perhaps once in a lifetime. The huge building was set to collapse magnificently and, to everyone's understanding, in a completely safe way.

No one even now is quite sure what went wrong, but went wrong it did. That day nine-year-old Katie Bender was killed and nine others were injured by flying debris from the hospital, which had exploded outwards rather than imploded as had been expected. More than 100,000 people watched as the hospital blew up and out towards the watching crowds, many not even realising that something had gone wrong until it was almost too late.

Neither I nor my family had been in attendance. Honestly, the whole thing sounded kind of odd to me, to watch destruction like that, and I just had a feeling it was better not to attend. Even so, it was a shock when we got the call that afternoon to attend the disaster control centre, which had suddenly been inundated with people who were frantic over their inability to contact loved ones who may have been at the site. We also played an active role in speaking with witnesses and collecting evidence from callers who had footage or were close to the site where the incident occurred.

Long days followed spent hearing people's stories and the accounts of their near-death experiences. It is hard to imagine how awful it was, as concrete and shrapnel flew across the water towards these vulnerable people. Some recalled being splattered not just with dust from the building but brain matter or body tissue from victims who had borne the brunt of the explosive impact. Their trauma intensified as their clothing was taken from them, collected as evidence for the inquest that would surely follow. I was grateful that none of my family had been in attendance, but I knew that no one in or around Canberra at that time escaped the impacts of the explosion as the images of those who died and were injured remained in the media and our imagination for weeks to come.

Working on disasters like these leave scars on first responders and care workers. Thankfully, the people in our team were well looked after for the weeks that followed, with our bosses ensuring we were debriefed after every shift and offered counselling. We looked after each other very well back then.

The days and weeks following the implosion were quite surreal. We worked side by side with the police and other professionals in the control centre, being part of the event as insiders. As we worked we looked up at numerous TVs all on different channels broadcasting the disaster. We sent police out to collect evidence and watched as evidence bags piled up and were taken for testing. All the while we talked with many people over the phone who just needed to talk about what they saw and heard and how they were feeling. I'll take simulated plane crashes any time, as opposed to the real thing.

Although I didn't know it then, as the world entered the first few years of the new millennium I was moving into a new part of my Dreaming. At first I was told there would be a restructure, which was hardly unusual for a public service that was constantly hiring expensive consultants who were employed to advise them on the best ways to save money. This was usually by paying their workers less and pulling back on the resources they needed to do their jobs. This time the consultants added that to prove we were doing a good job we should all re-apply for the jobs we were already doing.

I had built my way up to the position of Aboriginal child protection manager, after managing the Aboriginal child protection unit for many years and often also the intake team. It was me who decided upon the urgency and the response required for every child safety concern that was reported to the southern regional office. I had been awarded a public service award for the work I had done in child protection, and had almost single-handedly created the Aboriginal child protection process and grown it to the point where it needed a manager. I held that position as manager for many years and felt the restructure with the promised pay rise was just a matter of process.

With my 10 years of child protection experience I felt reasonably confident as I sat before the interview panel, which consisted of the new regional manager and a number of other Aboriginal professionals and community representatives. I answered all the questions and felt that the interview had gone quite well. It was the public service, so you can never be 100 per cent sure about any outcome, but I knew there was unlikely to be anyone else who could beat me for my position. I wasn't even nervous as we waited for the news to filter down about who had been awarded what roles, but my heart began to sink as I saw many competent and impressive colleagues lose their management positions and be relegated back down to case worker roles.

I couldn't quite believe what I was hearing: what were the consultants basing these decisions on? We were losing some of the most experienced people in the department, and I had no idea who was supposed to replace them. Still, I thought, they couldn't replace me, because who would have anything like my experience?

My turn came and I walked into the regional manager's office to hear the outcome. He smiled at me and I relaxed, relieved that at least my position was safe. 'You did a fantastic interview,' the regional manager began. 'The interview panel was extremely impressed and you certainly have a huge amount of experience. You should be very proud of what you have achieved in this role and in Aboriginal child protection more generally.'

I nodded. The words sounded positive, but a worm of doubt started squirming in my stomach. Something felt wrong.

'The thing is, Melinda,' he said, changing tack, 'the interview panel has decided that it's time to go in a different direction, to have a bit of new blood so to speak. You have done a great job over the last five years as the manager, there's no denying it, and we think it would be fantastic if you took on a more hands-on role as a caseworker.'

I was speechless. I had fought for years to get the Aboriginal child protection unit to even exist, and the management of it had now been taken away. I asked who would be taking the management role and my dismay grew: it had been awarded to a woman who had absolutely no experience in child protection. She did, however, have a high media profile as an Aboriginal advocate, which was what mattered apparently – not working hard behind the scenes to actually get things done.

I had to swallow my bitter disappointment. I decided that going back to being a caseworker was actually not a bad move. Being responsible for all the decisions made for Aboriginal children and families across all of Canberra was a huge amount of stress in an already stressful organisation, and returning to being a caseworker would allow me to spend time with my family, who really mattered. Soon I had completely accepted the decision and was looking forward to the new role.

When it was announced that every Aboriginal child in care should be returned to their parents, I couldn't believe what I was hearing. The children we had in care were subject to children's court orders for their protection, and even if I wanted to return them we would be violating the law to do so. My refusal to simply obey orders didn't go down well with management. There were complaints about me and even claims that I wasn't a real Aboriginal!

The validity of someone's Aboriginality had become somewhat political within the previous few decades. As recognition of Aboriginal legitimacy and rights started to become more mainstream there was also an increase in public profile for those who set themselves up as advocates for the community. Because of the continuing impacts of the Stolen Generations and the difficulties of tracing and documenting ancestry for those children taken from their homes and their descendants, it could be difficult to truly evidence a linear line of descent with Aboriginal heritage.

Self-identity and community recognition was the way in which this was ultimately resolved. Those with ties to a community or who could show they had Aboriginal heritage could assert their Aboriginality through means of a statutory declaration and a validation from an Aboriginal Elder. It isn't a perfect system, but it was the best available in a world where colonisation had smashed apart so many family bonds within Aboriginal communities. It also led to some infighting and jockeying for position as some within the communities and their advocates claimed others were not true Aboriginals, particularly if they had opinions or politics that did not align with those held by more powerful members of the political elite.

When I heard myself referred as not being Aboriginal I knew it was just a tactic to undermine my legitimacy in my role and try to prevent me from speaking out against the new procedures, which I felt were detrimental to the children in our care. However, it felt personal, like my very soul had been ripped from my body and stomped on. It was an insult not just to me, but to my mother and all her family. I picked up my bag and walked out of my office, having no idea what I would do or how Allen and I could continue to afford our mortgage.

As I walked across the car park towards my car a random thought floated into my head. I didn't know it then, but this was the ancestors once again directing me along my path. A strong and clear voice that spoke directly to my conscious mind said: 'Real estate.' I thought to myself, 'That sounds like something I'd like to do.' Abracadabra, the next day I had an interview with a local realtor and embarked on the next stage of my Dreaming: as a real estate agent.

27. A TURN IN THE PATH

Changing a name does not
change who we are.

– Unknown

I was now Mel to my new friends: it was my initiation into real estate. Melinda was gone, and only my older friends called me that and still do. My mum was horrified when she began to hear me called Mel and over the years she began to accept it, but still refuses to use it.

The next few years were a bit of a blur. I was working in real estate and found I was good at it. I was kicking goals and earning really good dollars, which suited me just fine. Then on 18 January 2003 Canberra was hit with the most horrifying firestorm in its history and my life took yet another turn.

Four days before the fire hit Canberra I was asked to do an appraisal on a property just south of Canberra in a small township called Tharwa. Me and my real estate partner were carrying out the appraisal on this home and property when I noticed activity down near the creek. The property owner said they were filling all the fire trucks and the Tharwa township was meeting that evening to arrange for all stock to be moved over the following few days.

I was a bit surprised: we had been following the fire updates for weeks and the fire was so far away that no one was the least bit concerned, but the farmer was adamant that come Friday or Saturday the fire would come over the mountains and nothing would stop it. There would be nothing left after it swept through.

Two days later as I sat in the office preparing for the day ahead I looked up to see thick smoke hanging over the street beyond my window. I could barely see 20 metres in front of me. Slightly panicked, I called Aunty Lynda, who had recently moved back to Canberra and was minding my daughters, and told her what I was seeing. We discussed the seriousness of the smoke and decided it was simply the wind pushing the smoke towards us from further away.

Feeling relieved, I went to my first open house of the day but after half an hour the smoke began to build again. After some increasingly concerned calls between me and the other agents we all decided it was time to pull up stumps and call it quits. I needed to get back to my kids and make sure everyone was okay. I rang Allen and told him I was heading home. He assured me that the fire wasn't going to get into the residential areas but something was telling me I had to get to my kids straight away, so I told him I was going to get them anyway. As I drove over the hill from Tuggeranong to Lanyon I could not fathom what I was seeing. My heart stopped and utter fear enveloped my body: in the distance a firestorm was rushing across the hills, causing what looked like explosions in its wake.

Time slowed as I pulled into Lynda's driveway and yelled for everyone to get into the car. Lynda was understandably distraught, terrified that she was going to lose her house. Thinking quickly, I gave the car keys to Lynda's daughter Tia, who was then around 19 years old, and told her to drive all the kids back to the relative safety of our home. Our home was located in South Canberra, which I thought was far enough from the firestorm to be fairly safe. 'If you hear anything about the fire coming close, you get them out and go straight to an evacuation centre,' I told her as all the kids piled into the car and she drove off. Determined to do what we could to save her home, Lynda and I stayed.

It was so surreal, standing waiting for that firestorm to rain down upon us. Inside I could hear the cricket being played on the television and outside all radios were tuned to the emergency services radio broadcast, which was advising everyone to stay in their homes because everything was under control. It didn't look as though it was under control.

Some of our neighbours switched their radios over to the local commercial channel, where they heard residents of nearby suburbs ringing in to the talkback and telling the host that their streets were literally on fire. There were stories of a service station exploding, trees bursting into flames and the sounds of fire alarms blaring as houses caught alight, falling like dominoes in the path of the fiery push of flames.

Around us the smoke became so thick that by early afternoon day had turned to night. The horizon became tinged with an eerie orange glow as the fire relentlessly marched towards us. The neighbours started to organise a kind of human telegraph system, as up and down the street they all stood on their rooftops watching the fire's approach. We were creating our own live rundown of the firestorm's progress as it descended. Those not on the rooves were preparing to run should the fire glow in the distance become burning embers raining down upon us.

For two to three hours we lived on the edge, our senses heightened to even the smallest wind change. The orange glow on the immediate horizon dimmed then re-ignited, giving and taking hope with each change – yet, over time somehow, it gradually faded and we knew that this street was one of the lucky ones, spared from the carnage that roared through Canberra that day. Throughout it all I could not understand why no one was talking to us, advising us what to do as the horizon continued to glow orange well into the night. Was the threat truly past, or should we be ever alert and ready to flee in the night as the storm of flame started to rage again? No one knew.

Most Canberrans spent the following week on high alert as small fires re-ignited or new fires began. More than once a family was found in their pyjamas out in the street as they rushed out of their homes because they had been told to be ready to evacuate over and over again, only to see that the fire was not near their neighbourhood. Many others were not so lucky, not receiving the warning in time and barely escaping with their lives as the fire descended.

The crisis lasted for more than four days, and by the time it was under control almost 500 people had been injured, four sadly losing their lives, 470 houses destroyed and almost 70 per cent of the ACT's pastoral and farm land decimated. Although the major firestorm was under control by 21 January it took weeks for the smoke to dissipate, causing additional concerns as people struggled with breathing issues and trying to deal with the devastation around them in the haze. Because of the damage to residential streets there was a huge demand in housing for those who had lost their homes. Every house that we had on the market was snapped up and prices started to soar.

As a real estate agent this benefited me and it was surely profitable, but I couldn't help thinking how predatory it seemed. Even when our agency pledged to donate $1,000 from every house sold towards the fire relief fund I still felt uncomfortable, profiting at such a terrible time. It hurt my soul in some unspoken but fundamental way. I was providing for my family, but how was I contributing to the world, how was I nourishing and caring for my spirit and the spirit of the world? In the ashes of that January fire I started to feel a new Dreaming rise, like a phoenix from the ashes.

The firestorm had been terrifying and the costs were still being tallied, yet part of me was in awe of what had just occurred. What I had witnessed was nothing less than an unmistakable display of the power of Mother Nature and what happens if you fail to pay her the respect she deserves. I realised that for so long I had been disconnected from the world around me, the natural ebb and flow and the healing and power that offers us. I recalled the feeling I had sitting by the dam on the sheep station back when I was a kid, how the spirit of the bush had helped me be calm and reconcile my emotions. I longed to feel that connection again, and I knew that the life I was living was not the one that was right for me. My ancestors were calling, and part of me could feel it pulling me in a new and unexpected direction.

Signs and portents were around me – losing my manager position, the firestorm, the sense of disconnection – but I still wasn't quite getting what the universe was trying to tell me. I was working in real estate and complaining and whining about it to anyone who would listen, but I was not yet brave enough to leave.

'It's not that they are bad people,' I explained to my girlfriend as we browsed through the shelves of the local bookstore, 'but real estate makes you act like a shark. It's ruthless and people can lose sight that they are dealing with real people.' She nodded in understanding of what I was saying. I wanted to leave; I just didn't know where to go or how to change my life. I had been through so much and finally had stability, a fantastic income and a strong and loving family. Why was I unhappy?

146

As I thought about this my eyes fell on a book placed on the shelf just above my friend's shoulder. I instinctively reached out for it and started reading the back cover: the book was about modern witchcraft. I didn't know anything about witches, witchcraft or paganism and had never read anything that dealt with those subjects, yet I felt compelled to buy this book and take it home.

Even though I may not have been experienced with the ideas of witchcraft and paganism I had always had a feeling that there was more going on in this world than what I was being taught and that I could physically see. I probably wouldn't have been able to describe my beliefs, but I knew even then that there was a Dreaming I had yet to travel to discover the true essence of me, my real self, and maybe this book was some kind of portal to that, to the world of my spiritual self that I had often glimpsed but had never really taken the time to get to know.

This book gave me a lot of the answers I was looking for, introducing me to the concept of paganism, the Rule of Three and the fact that what you put out in the world comes back to you. As I read the words I realised I had been experiencing these things my whole life. Witchcraft and the ideas it engaged with were speaking to me, not to tell me fresh information but to remind me of things I already knew.

As I began to openly embrace these ideas I developed new connections with people who were part of the pagan and witchcraft community in Canberra. It was surprising how many people there were who lived and thought like this, their lives made richer and more meaningful by ritual and a conscious connection with nature.

Some years later I moved away from Canberra and a dear friend of mine, a well-respected Aboriginal Elder, passed away, so I travelled to Queanbeyan to attend her funeral. The service was carried out in true Catholic tradition, something that was remarkably common among Aboriginal communities due to the historical connection of Catholic missionaries and missions. Although many of these connections led to a disconnect between our Aboriginal peoples and their Countries and extended families, those who found themselves in missions or religious organisations gravitated to the rituals and spiritual aspects of Catholic traditions. I had been schooled for several years in a Catholic school, and my mother had attended Catholic school and had been expected to become a nun.

The link between religious rituals and Aboriginal spirituality was one that I had never really thought about as a child, but after connecting with the witchcraft and pagan traditions I was learning I started to think about how often Christian and other institutional religions had used ancient spiritual knowledge, ideas and sites to establish and legitimise their own practices.

While listening to my friend's funeral rites I was struck by how formal and dry the elements were, with everyone sitting and watching quietly as a few anointed people orchestrated the elaborate recitals of prayer and determined the rituals of the funeral rites. I began to wonder why my friend, an Aboriginal Elder and someone so connected to Aboriginal culture, would have opted for a burial like that. I expressed my annoyance with a girlfriend who was also attending the funeral, and she shook her head in wonderment.

'Really, you don't see it?' I didn't know what she was talking about. 'They just put it under a roof, that's all,' she responded. When we had left the church she said, 'All those rituals, the reverence, the incense, the connection with spirit: it's just the same thing but in a different package. Rituals are universal, they connect us with spirit, but we all have our own ways to understand and create our pathways to that universal energy. Ancient pagan rituals and Aboriginal belief systems value the earth and spirit and see all these things as connected. The Catholic traditions interpreted this as the ashes to ashes, dust to dust litany. We come from the earth and we go back to the earth. It's the same message, just a slightly different language.'

I looked at my girlfriend in wonder as I realised this was something profound. While we focus on difference, on how our religions, customs or history differ, we miss the great thing that unites us all: our shared connection with spirit. Instead of seeing this funeral as something artificial and performative, I suddenly saw it was simply a different way of demonstrating what we all share. Through her passing, my dear friend made me realise something that was obvious to me all along if only I had truly looked at it. She found her way through to this world and connected with spirit through her religious beliefs, but she had not dictated anyone else do so.

She had presented me with one more important lesson before departing this world: that you can integrate many ideas and find meaning. I could integrate both my Aboriginal and white heritage into a belief system that had room for varied beliefs and different understandings. It was a revelation, and I soon found myself becoming deeply connected with the old ways of both cultures through practising and designing my own spellwork and rituals.

I was gripped with a desire to show the world these connections, although I really didn't know exactly how I was going to do that quite yet.

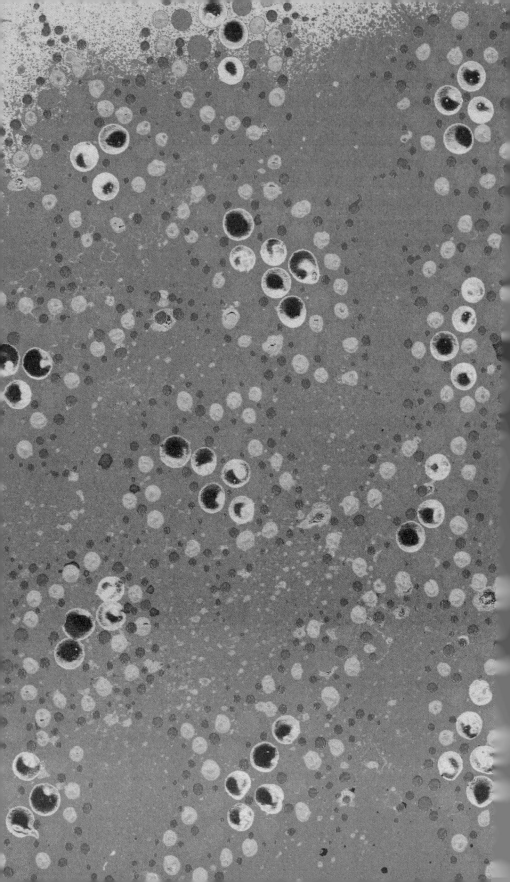

28. SIGNS FROM THE UNIVERSE

*To be a witch is to know the
power of your own magick.*

– UNKNOWN

Witchcraft and paganism have traditionally been demonised by Christian traditions, linking them to Satanism and a lack of civilised ideas. Many of these same condemnations were levelled against Aboriginal cultural practices, and I could see the correlations between the two different spiritual paths. People think spells are some kind of negative evil practice, when really more generally spells and magic are nothing more than positive affirmations that are conducted as part of rituals. They are more like prayers than they are anything demonic or evil.

Engaging in spellcraft helps me become more organised and focused on working towards the outcome I want, and lets the universe know I am listening and trying to work in harmony with it. Whenever I feel lost, disconnected or confused the tools offered by spellwork and ritual help me find the right path.

I certainly felt lost back then. Things in the real estate office were going poorly. I needed to list and sell two houses per month to achieve my target, and I had been finding that almost impossible. I wasn't quite ready to leave my job even though I could feel myself being pulled away from it. Instead, I decided to use spellwork and positive affirmations to try to improve my situation. It worked almost immediately, as my sales improved and I easily met my next targets.

My magic work was helping me, but I knew it still didn't feel right. I was avoiding doing the thing I knew I had to do, and that never works out well even when you have magical tools to help you do it. One thing I had learned through all of my experiences in life is that if you continue to work against your best interests and true self and make decisions that may seem fine financially or save you having to deal with an uncomfortable truth but do nothing to nourish your soul, then the universe will find a way of forcing change in ways that are rarely pleasant or easy.

I knew I couldn't stay in the job or that life forever even if things were improving, so I got brave and decided it was time to put my money where my mouth was and take at least one small step in the right direction. I opened a small stall at a local market, just on a Sunday, where I sold all things alternative: crystals, spell kits, statues, incense and other pagan products. The markets brought in some good money, but they also showed me I had a real affinity for that kind of life. I gained confidence in what I was learning and became a part of the larger pagan community, creating strong links and friendships I still hold to this day. I was slowly transitioning from one life to the next, and a new Dreaming was unfurling without me being aware it was happening.

As my spirit started to blossom I found it harder and harder to go into the real estate office. I walked across the threshold with a sense of dread, wondering if that was going to be the day the Rule of Three was going to get me, finally deciding that enough was enough. How long was I going to be able to deny that my job was totally wrong for me, that it was in the way of me becoming who I was supposed to be? How long before the universe decided it was going to push me rather than patiently give me signs to exit gracefully?

I have a deep and profound respect for the ideas of paganism and understand why and how they work in connection with your true spirit, but that old threefold law has always scared the hell out of me. I knew that it was tallying up what I was doing and it was going to return it in spades. To survive in real estate you have to be a profiteer, you have to be unethical and you have to be more focused on money than people. I was swimming with sharks and sooner or later, if I didn't get out, I would have to end up being a shark or being eaten alive by them.

I finally decided it was time to get out of the shark-infested water and get onto dry land, and I mentally let the universe know I was ready and asked to be sent a sign and stated I would follow it. As is so often the case, the universe chose a surprising path to lead me towards my new Dreaming.

I had been walking to my car after leaving my child protection career when the idea of being a real estate agent had occurred to me, and once again I was in a car park after handing in my resignation as a real estate agent when a solicitor who I referred work to offered me a receptionist job at her solicitor's office. I have no idea why she thought I would be looking for a job or why I would move from the profitable world of real estate to a low-paid receptionist position, but I took the offer on the spot.

The new job was only part time, and although it meant a huge step down financially I suddenly found I had the time and energy to truly focus on growing my market business into a viable source of income. More importantly, I found myself in a place where I could breathe easily, knowing that I was finally listening to my spirit and the universe would have no reason to want to give me a nasty wake-up call with that pesky threefold law.

As I opened myself up to my new Dreaming I started to notice I had a surprisingly sensitive ability to 'know' things. It wasn't just recognising my feelings when I was doing things out of sync with the universe and my best self, but when the universe had messages to tell me I found I could recognise and understand them. I started to trust my gut feelings, which were really my ability to read the energy around me, and I started to understand that when I had known things in my past I was connecting with the greater realm and not just being crazy or making things up, as I had constantly been accused as a child and young adult. I no longer questioned that the universe really did speak to me, and as a result I strengthened my ability to listen to it and discovered I was clairsentient.

'Clairsentience' is clear feeling, and it is the way to describe the ability to feel the energy of others and read them and their desires, futures and best life paths. I started to learn the tarot, and found it an excellent tool through which I could connect with the energy all around me in a targeted way. A thought started to bubble away at the back of my mind. The tarot is an ancient Indo-European tool that has been used since the Middle Ages across the northern hemisphere, and the cards, which contain symbolic references to a number of spiritual, historical and psychological elements, are a useful tool to give shape and form to the energetic messages around us when properly examined and interpreted by someone with psychic abilities. Could there be a form of these cards that was more closely attuned not with a European history, but a history and understanding of this land that my Aboriginal ancestors had inhabited for thousands of years?

It was just a thought then, but a persistent one.

As I started to really embrace my spirituality I noticed I was not the only member of my family who was engaging with the world of spirit. A year earlier in 2002 Allen and I had built a new house in a sought-after and rather affluent part of Gordon, in the district of Tuggeranong in Canberra. After we moved in my eldest daughter Teniel, who was around 12 years of age, started going through a particularly difficult time, erupting into violent outbursts and overwrought emotional reactions to the tiniest things.

Puberty can be particularly difficult on girls as they move from the stage of girlhood into womanhood, with all the physical, social and psychological repercussions of that transition, but as Teniel's behaviour worsened I began to realise that it was not just puberty, that something else was going on: something deeper. My daughter had often challenged our parenting but was then out of control, and neither Allen nor I could work out how best to deal with it. It wasn't just Teniel: I noticed we all seemed to be on edge, nervous and reactive, although Teniel was certainly exhibiting the worst of it.

After one particularly awful confrontation we decided it was best for Teniel to stay with her grandparents for a few days until we had calmed down and could talk with her rationally and without emotion. We wondered if Teniel needed some kind of therapy or perhaps to live away from us because it had got so bad, but I knew instinctively this wasn't about Teniel – at least, not totally. Something else was going on and I could feel it, but I didn't know how to identify or deal with it.

While Teniel was away I decided to invite two of my friends, Sandy and Denise, to check out my new house and give me their opinions on what might be happening and why our family, particularly Teniel, seemed so unsettled and unhappy. These women were very spiritually connected, having been involved with the psychic and spiritual community for years, and I had found their insights and understanding of the spiritual realm to be both astounding and eerily accurate as our relationship developed. Something had been telling me that Teniel's behaviour was not just the result of out-of-control hormones, and I knew if anyone could throw some light on any spiritual disturbances then Denise and Sandy could.

I didn't tell them about my suspicions before they arrived, just that I had been having some trouble with my eldest daughter and really wanted them to have a look around. It was a new house so it didn't have any previous history to speak of, so it further perplexed me as to what was going on. We had a chat and I told them about the outbursts and poor behaviour, and Sandy suggested we check out the house to see if they could sense any energetic issues or blockages anywhere that could be causing Teniel's unsettlement. We went from room to room, and Sandy and Denise noticed nothing concerning until they arrived at the doorway to Teniel's bedroom. There they stopped, silent and tense.

'Do you hear that?' Sandy asked. I shook my head; I couldn't hear anything.

'It's a baby crying,' Denise answered and the two of them nodded, as though it was the most obvious answer in the world.

'It's really distressed,' Sandy explained to me. 'I can't imagine how anyone could get any sleep in this room with the way that child is wailing, almost without a breath.'

Try as I might I couldn't hear a baby crying, but my friends felt drawn to the middle of the room and constantly glanced up at the ceiling and then looked at each other.

'Do you see it?' Sandy asked Denise.

Denise nodded. 'I feel it too.' The two women looked at me gravely.

'There's a portal here,' Sandy told me. 'That's where the sound is coming through. We need to close it.'

Anyone else may have been sceptical of this declaration, but during my time discovering the craft I had come to understand that different people had different gifts. Even though I couldn't hear a baby I had no doubt that my friends heard it, so I readily agreed to their request to

155

form a magical circle and work together to close the portal. It worked, but I couldn't help but wonder why a portal had opened in the first place and why it had chosen to do so in my eldest daughter's room.

The following day I collected Teniel from her nan's house. She seemed different: less emotional and more like her old self. I decided to broach the subject with her and asked whether she ever heard anything in her bedroom. I didn't mention anything about the baby or a portal from another dimension; after all, I didn't want her to think I had gone mad. As soon as the question had been asked my daughter broke into tears, telling me about the awful crying of the baby that kept her up night after night.

As Teniel spoke about the noises that had agitated her so much I realised she had not been acting out because of nastiness or a hormone imbalance, but that she had been exhausted and frightened by the energetic disturbance in her room and had no way to tell us about it. There had been no words or understanding to explain it without, as she said, looking 'crazy'. The few days at her grandparents' house when she got some real rest and then the opportunity to tell me about the true reason for her anger and distress were what she had needed the whole time.

I hugged her, noting how the fear of being crazy was such a barrier to us being able to talk about the experience we had had. I had felt the same concern myself and had hesitated to ask my daughter about it, fearing she would think me mad. How close I had come to missing out on an opportunity to solve my child's distress, and I vowed that I would never let the fear that others thought I was crazy stop me from telling the truth about the experiences I had or stop me helping others whom I suspected were experiencing the same thing.

'It's okay, baby,' I told her, comforting her in my arms. 'I had some friends, Sandy and Denise, come over and they heard the baby too.'

Teniel looked up at me then, hope and relief in her eyes. 'They did?'

I nodded. 'Yes, and they knew just what to do about it. You won't have to hear that crying anymore. It's all over now.' She hugged me tightly, and I knew her relief wasn't just because the endless crying may finally have stopped but that I believed her when she told me about it. 'Sweetheart,' I said, softly, stroking her hair, 'if you ever experience anything strange or that you don't understand you can tell me about it, okay? I will always believe you. I know there is more to this world than what the average person sees and experiences.'

Teniel nodded and then in a tiny voice said, 'There's also a man, a strange man in a suit. He carries a briefcase and he's always at the bus stop in the morning when I go to school, but no one else can see him.' She looked up at me, still fearing that I may not believe her.

'Do you see anyone else?'

Teniel nodded. 'Yes, there was this clown and he sometimes follows me at school. He just appears out of nowhere, but no one else sees him and he scares me.'

I thought about this for a long moment. 'I think you are what we call a seer, or a clairvoyant. Part of that is that you can see people who have passed away, or remnants of their spirits at least. They can appear to be people the same as everyone else, but somehow you know they're not. We call them "solids" because they look like ordinary human beings, but only very sensitive people can see them.'

'Do you see them too?' Teniel asked. I shook my head: I have never possessed that particular gift, but I knew from my own experiences of connecting with the other world through my new interest in witchcraft, tarot and intuitive healing that it could be a scary ability to deal with. I decided then and there to help teach my daughter how to protect herself from these uninvited apparitions.

As the years passed and Teniel grew older she continued to see ghosts and spirits, but she always managed to deal with them without fear and with a kind of dignified pragmatism. She gave them her own special words, the 'hitchhikers' and the 'visitors'. We often had conversations about new ones or old friends she saw during her day, making the whole experience one she could share and therefore make far less threatening or upsetting.

My other daughters had their own special gifts to differing degrees. My youngest, Jenna, saw faeries a lot when she was a small child. Once in an effort to understand what she was seeing I brought home a friend who had a strong connection to that spiritual realm, and the two of them chatted happily about a faerie who was playing on the windowsill in front of them. I couldn't see anything, but from the way they were talking it was clear they had a very clear view of a little fae person prancing about and engaging with them. Unfortunately, as she grew older Jenna's ability to see the faery realm faded, and by the time she was an adult she never spoke of conversing with her faery friends.

My middle daughter, Cassie-lee, was the opposite. She showed no intuitive or psychic abilities as a child, but as she aged she started to have a chilling ability to predict car accidents and fatalities. She always seemed to know if we were heading towards a place where an accident was about to happen and became quite proficient at attending to people at the scene, because she was so often the first one to get to them.

That was what it was like being part of our clan. Other families bonded over football or TV shows they liked, while we talked about dead people, faeries and car accidents.

29. MAGICKAL REALM

And just like magic, it's gone.

– UNKNOWN

My marriage to Allen had been a revelation at the beginning. Being with someone who loved and respected me in a relationship not characterised by violence or turmoil changed me and the way I saw myself. I developed confidence that I was a worthy person, and my love for my children and husband was unquestioned. Even as everything around me changed I truly believed that my marriage and family life were no longer areas where I had to have any concerns. Been there, done that.

Our relationship was based on a strong and profound trust, a belief that no matter what Allen would have my back. I was so secure in the belief that he felt the same. It is true that over time Allen and I had fallen into the usual mundane relationship a lot of married people find themselves in, our conversations revolving around the kids or casual information about work or a particular social event. It was nothing terribly deep but that was normal. Allen worked for his parents, I worked, and we had two cars and a nice house and never put much thought into wondering if life could be different. I truly believed we were life partners – until I found the text messages.

I have to be clear: as far as I knew Allen had not been cheating on me. The texts between him and his female co-worker were in no way sexual, but what I read in these was to my mind so much worse. The information he was sharing had such a depth of feeling; he had told her things that I felt were too close to being intimate. What they were discussing went so far beyond the connections you share in a physical relationship and, I was appalled to see, they were sharing up to 50 text messages a day. I could not help but feel hurt and betrayed.

Knowing so many of these texts existed was like a gut punch, and from someone who loved you and seemed genuinely confused about why this blow had hurt you. Allen insisted that he still loved me and I wanted our marriage to succeed, so the two of us did what many people in failing marriages do: we ignored the problem by running away from it. We built a new house and filled our lives with holidays and material possessions, focusing our time and thoughts on anything except the problem between us. Of course this never works, and despite our every effort to pretend that the problem didn't exist, each day my feelings of mistrust created a distance between us. Allen was a good, generous and devoted husband and he tried desperately to prove his love to me, but as hard as I fought against it the damage was just too much for me to recover from.

How could it be that Allen and I were wrong for each other, that our marriage was not the right path for me? He had loved me in a way that showed me what love could be, and we had three beautiful children and had built a life together.

While I worried about my marriage and contemplated my next steps the universe was already starting to show me a solution. I began to notice that my market stall was becoming increasingly successful: I had a strong and stable group of customers, and the items and services I was offering were in high demand. I started to think that maybe I could turn this stall into a proper business, perhaps a shop offering alternative therapies, readings, products and services? Despite the success of my stall I felt that Canberra was a bit too conservative to sustain a full New Age shop. Many before had not succeeded, and I didn't want to be another statistic.

I had lived in Canberra for most of my life, but as the problems between Allen and me intensified I felt myself being tugged. The idea of starting again somewhere new became undeniable, and I wanted to get away: away from Canberra and, most importantly, away from this other woman. I knew she was in our past, but I was always aware that I could easily bump into her in a supermarket or at a social event. I needed to run away from everything that reminded me of the hurt and betrayal I felt, and it was everywhere I looked. If we could get away we could find ourselves again. The trouble was that I had no idea how or where to start, and as I became increasingly discontented I sat down to write a new spell to help direct me towards my future Dreaming.

Having completed my spell on the right day and at the right time of the moon cycle, I simply asked, 'Where do I need to go?' That night I awoke at 2 am with the word 'Ballina' in my head. I woke Allen and said, 'We're moving to Ballina.'

He just looked at me groggily for a moment, said 'Okay,' then rolled over.

After a moment I roused him again. 'Where exactly is Ballina?' He shook his head and fell back asleep.

Two months after crafting my spell Allen and I packed up the house and moved to Ballina, which it turned out was on the far north coast of New South Wales. It's a small beach town that serves as a handy tourist stop for those travelling up from Sydney to the Queensland border and beyond.

We found the most amazing little shop on the main street, an old house that had been converted into a shop after the town had become more prosperous. It was a good size, with a reasonable-sized shopfront for stock and three rooms that could be rented out to therapists, so we could offer a large range of natural and alternative therapies. The minute I saw it I knew it was perfect.

I named the shop Magickal Realm and couldn't wait to open for business. It wasn't long before it became my whole world: my business, social scene and personal sanctuary, where I could be as weird and wonderful as I liked and never had to explain myself to anyone. Amazingly, I found there were a lot of people just like me and Magickal Realm soon became the spiritual and magical hub of my little coastal town.

We had our share of notable guests to the shop, some human and some not so human. On one occasion the well-known psychic medium Charmaine Wilson unexpectedly walked in. I recognised her immediately, as she had just won a national television psychic reality show called *The One* and I was a huge fan of her abilities and gentle, down-to-earth nature. I knew she was touring the coast but her venues were large cities, not tiny towns like Ballina, and I never dreamed she would ever be in my humble little shop.

Charmaine is best known for her ability to talk with those who have passed and share messages for loved ones still living. As she saw me at the counter she came over to me and grasped my hand, her palms soft and gentle as she smiled at me and said without any preamble, 'I just want you to know there is a little old lady around you. She is a very protective spirit. I think her name is Tess . . . or . . . No, it's Bess, her name is Bess.'

My mouth dropped to the floor. My beloved Nanna Bess, who had loved me so much as a child, had passed away many years ago and there was rarely a day I didn't miss her. To hear her name spoken by this acclaimed medium without any request or coaxing seemed like validation that she was still, even then, watching over me.

'She has been watching for some time,' Charmaine assured me. 'Did she pass just a little before the birth of a child?' I nodded. Nanna Bess had died just a few months before I knew I was pregnant with Cassie-lee. Charmaine smiled and said, 'She is showing me a pebble: does that mean anything to you?'

I shook my head, not in defiance but in surprise. How could Charmaine have known, as I had not told anyone this story yet here I was being reminded of it. It had happened just a few days after Nanna Bess had passed away. I was grief stricken and depressed and I am sorry to say quick to get irritable at even the smallest things. That day I had been caught at a set of damn lights on my way that were refusing to change. I sat there while minutes passed and still the light remained stubbornly red.

I was getting more and more irritated. It was late and there was not a single other car in sight, but still those lights wouldn't change. I was thinking about just running through them when I heard a sound on the roof of the car. There was nothing around me, the sky was clear and there was not another soul in the world, but still I heard the noise and then watched as a tiny pebble rolled lazily off my roof and down the windscreen directly in front of me, making its way slowly onto the bonnet and then disappearing onto the road. There was nowhere this pebble could have come from and no reason for it to have rolled down my car. It made no sense, but somehow I knew it was a message from Nanna Bess – although I had no idea what she was trying to say.

Six weeks later I discovered I was pregnant and I just knew the pebble had been Nanna Bess's way of letting me know that she was still around and that she was watching over me and my children. After the nurse had told me how far along I was I realised that Nanna Bess was also letting me know I had just fallen pregnant with my own little pebble, now inside me.

My brief meeting with Charmaine had a lasting effect on me, because she confirmed that the spirit world, through Nanna Bess, was watching over me and my children and that my beloved nanna would always be there for me no matter how tough things might get – and times were getting tough. Our move was great in a lot of ways and I loved the shop and new community I was discovering, but my marriage wasn't improving as much as I had hoped it would and running a spiritual store full time was exhausting and time consuming. Added to this, there was no shortage of people who felt the need to come into my space to let me know how silly or evil or misguided I was to be dealing with the spirit world, while others treated the whole thing with utter disrespect.

There was one particular woman who came into the store for a tarot reading and spent the entire time arguing with me and telling me I was wrong. I didn't know what to say to her as I was fairly clear about the messages I was getting, but still she resisted until finally I had to politely suggest we finish up the reading and I would refund her the fee. At that point everything changed and the woman suddenly broke down, confessing that everything I had said was actually true but she really didn't want it to be. She asked me to continue the reading and came back several times afterwards. Every time I read for her she was resistant and belligerent until finally she broke down and cried. It was exhausting, but that was the thing about Magickal Realms: it was a place where everyone was welcome and many were drawn even if they didn't know exactly why they needed to be there.

Magickal Realm was more than just a shop. It was a place for the spiritual community to gather, and it was not uncommon for there to be three or four people sitting in my office having strange and extraordinary conversations. We talked about everything from past lives to tarot reading, connecting with angels, numerology, astrology and crystal classes. We even had people telling us about their experiences with alien abduction!

Tony and Olga didn't seem like your usual alien conspiracy theorists. They were quite elderly with greying hair, huge smiles and welcoming embraces yet they insisted they had not just experienced being abducted by aliens, but that it had happened to them several times. Their first experience of UFO abduction had occurred out of the blue one night while they were driving in the middle of Sydney, a very busy city on Australia's east coast. As they were driving their car was picked up by a passing space ship and Tony was held by aliens for a period of time.

Olga was left sitting in the car, alone and terrified, not knowing where her husband Tony was. Tony never went into detail about where he had been during his absence, but he did allude to things being done to him by his alien captors before moving on with the rest of the amazing story.

Once the aliens were finished with their business the couple was returned to earth, seemingly none the worse for wear but many kilometres away from where they had originally been abducted. Olga and Tony swore that no physical earth time had passed since they had been picked up even though they had been in the spaceship for at least a few hours, and driving from Sydney to the place where they ended up would have taken an hour at least.

That was Olga's only first-hand experience of abduction but Tony was removed many times, usually from his bed in the middle of the night. Tony said he had given 'them' permission to experiment on him, although he never explained why such permission had been sought or given or what it was permission to do. Each morning after a visitation and abduction Olga awoke next to Tony to find him covered in small skin-like bandaids on parts of his body that had not been there when he had gone to sleep the previous evening and were like nothing she had ever been able to find in any store.

Tony's stories were detailed and disturbing, and most people who heard them couldn't help but be convinced by the earnest way in which he provided the information. He offered to teach the participants how to open themselves up for more easy contact with aliens. I wasn't having a bar of that because the whole thought of being taken up into the heavens by creatures from a distant world scared the crap out of me, but a good number of people were interested enough that we arranged to have a class and informational session at Magickal Realm, where Tony would take anyone who was foolhardy enough to try through the process he used to communicate with these visitors from another planet. Several people who attended the class experimented with his instructions and a few came back to class talking about their experiences.

I might not have been communing with Tony's aliens, but I was encountering my own strange experiences and visitations inside Magickal Realms. In the hallway leading off to our treatment rooms our staff and customers often complained about a distinctly cold, uncomfortable spot they tried to avoid walking through. After much conversation we decided to investigate further and, using a dowsing rod, we found a spirit portal in that very spot. I knew all about portals and the trouble they could cause thanks to the one we had encountered in my daughter's bedroom, but still I was sceptical. After all, how many interdimensional or spirit portals could there possibly be?

Kevin, who had found the portal with his dowsing rod, was adamant that it was there, and to prove it he took a glass of water and poured it directly into the spot he claimed the portal was situated. Astoundingly, the timber floor in that area dried up almost as soon as the water hit the floor, yet any drops that spilled out beyond that exact spot formed clear pools of water. I was convinced, and we created a cleansing ritual and performed it immediately. The next day when testing whether our ritual had worked we again poured water on the same site, and this time there was a big old puddle of water sitting there that I then had to mop up.

You would think with things like this going on that Magickal Realms might be a scary place to be, but it wasn't. It was when I was at home, lying in bed at night and worrying about the finances that I felt real fear. While the shop had attracted a terrific bunch of people and was offering a great service to the alternative community, I just couldn't seem to make any real money. I know a lot of people say that money isn't everything and that is true, but it is important. Money buys choices and freedom and opportunities. I had spent my childhood and early adult life having none of those things, and I was fearful that I would yet again end up in a situation where I was unable to make my own choices and determine my own fate.

It also didn't help that I was at that point pretty much managing everything on my own. Although Allen had originally made the move with me, he decided to go back to Canberra to settle a few things and finish off his job. I was left in Ballina running the business and raising the girls all on my own. Allen eventually returned to us in Ballina, but the separation had put further strain on our already fragile relationship. Although we were happy to have him back, it never felt like we returned to being the family we had been. I was in a strange emotional state, neither happy nor unhappy but just going through the routine of living life and trying not to think about the issues that were quickly gathering like a thunderstorm around me.

Allen was a good dad and was certainly putting in a lot of effort to make things work between us, so I didn't really have any reason to leave him and we both wanted to be there for the raising of our children. I knew deep down, however, that this was not going to last.

30. FINDING MICHAEL - AGAIN

My favourite witch. Maybe you didn't get it so wrong.

– MICHAEL

Change comes in the strangest ways, especially for me, and I had no warning about exactly how my world was going to change around me once again.

It was a day in early December when the universe decided to start putting the changes it had been planning all along into motion. It seemed like any other day, really: I was at the shop doing some paperwork and I heard someone come through the door of Magickal Realm. Shortly afterwards one of my staff came into my office red faced and irritated.

'Can you deal with this idiot?' she asked, pointing to the shop floor and then walking off towards the treatment rooms. I went out to see what was going on. Staff at Magickal Realm were famously resilient and tolerant, so for someone to annoy one of my girls meant it was probably going to be a quite difficult customer.

I was surprised to see that the man who stood out on the shop floor looked fairly ordinary. He was tall and solid, with big hands and an energy that you felt as soon as you stepped into the room with him. He seemed familiar, but I didn't know why. As soon as he saw me he started making smart-arse comments, asking me whether I was going to turn him into a frog and lightheartedly making fun of things. He may have thought he was being hilarious, but no one else did. I shook my head at his attempt at being funny and he then asked what I did, to which I replied: 'Tarot.'

Tarot is not an easy tool to work with: it takes a long time to learn the symbolism of the cards and how they work together, and to understand and know what spreads are the best at what kinds of questions. It takes longer still to absorb all of that and then let it go and trust your intuitive nature. It also takes experience to understand that the symbolic and historical meanings of the cards are just the way in which to familiarise yourself with the magical ways in which they connect with other realms, and that the only way to understand the real messages they are trying to share is to trust your connection with them to guide your intuition to the right answers.

Patience and skill are needed to empty your mind of all the noise and make space to see, listen and know the messages being shared with you by spirit. This is a hard place to be for any length of time, as it requires you to be in two places at once: both the timeless place of spirit and the here and now of everyday life, which is why not every reading feels the same. Sometimes you get an instant connection and sometimes it is just hard work.

I suspected that in dealing with this buffoon and his weak attempts at humour it was much more likely to be the latter, and I hoped he would scoff at the suggestion of me doing a reading and leave the shop – but he didn't. I took him into the reading room and started shuffling the cards, completely unaware that this reading would impact the rest of my life. This good old Aussie bloke introduced himself as Michael: not Mike or Mick but Michael. We settled into my reading room and I was quickly overwhelmed by the visions that came fast and clear. The visions revealed that this man had been my lover in a previous life.

I didn't know what to do with this revelation. He certainly didn't seem like the kind of bloke who would take any of this seriously, yet my intuition was telling me I should share what I was picking up with him. I have to trust this intuitive voice, so despite my reservations I began to tell him what I was seeing.

'I think I am picking up on a previous life we may have shared together,' I said, not daring to look up expecting some smart comment or wisecrack. Michael didn't say anything and I continued on, moving my reading into present tense as the man's past played in front of me like a movie. 'I think you were a Quaker, a leader in the community.

You're fair, just and well liked but strict, and you rule with an iron fist.' He smiled and I felt the pressure in the reading room ease greatly.

'You are also the town executioner. You make sure that the moral codes of the township are followed to the letter. But you are also having an affair with a younger, married woman,' I said, 'and she isn't married to you.' Michael laughed, but it wasn't a humorous laugh like the one he had given me in the front of the shop. It was more like a laugh of recognition. 'And that woman,' I continued, 'was me.'

I paused for a moment, not sure what his reaction would be. He was looking at me steadily, not saying a word, so I blundered on. The images I was getting were coming so fast yet I felt disconnected from my words. 'We are in love but we must keep it a secret, so we meet after dark and in out of the way places. We think we are being discreet, but we are observed and called out by others in the community.' Emotion began to ebb its way in as I felt again what I had felt in this past life. 'I am banished from our township and I never saw you again.'

I looked up then as the visions faded and realised that what I had just said must have sounded crazy to this man, but he wasn't laughing. To my absolute surprise, Michael reached across and took my hand in his. He looked me in the eyes and said, 'I don't know what the hell that was all about, but I feel it too.'

Our hands separated, and to cover my shame I quickly explained: 'This is from a life already gone, not now,' I said. 'It's a shared soul connection that for some reason is coming up again here, which is why we met.'

'A shared soul connection?'

I shrugged. 'Sometimes, like now, people energetically resonate with one another and can still have a very deep connection from lives and experiences they had lived hundreds of years ago. We reincarnate together over many life times, and our souls recognise each other even though our physical appearances change. These are soul connections, or members of a soul group. It's like when you meet someone and you feel as though you've known them forever but you've only just met them.'

I somehow found my professionalism and got back to the job at hand. I continued with Michael's reading, taking much more of an interest in the reading than I should have.

Over the following weeks Michael visited the shop regularly, and we continued our talks about spirit, past lives and soul connections. He decided to join one of our meditation classes and a few of the discussion master classes on past lives as an energetic connection. We became friends, with absolutely no thought of moving our relationship beyond the bounds of friendship.

I was married and Michael was in a relationship, though he was not taking it very seriously. 'Friends with benefits' he called it, though I would often suggest that the woman he was seeing may in fact see it as something more intimate. He continually said he had been honest with her from the start about not being willing or able to give her more. As our friendship quickly blossomed we shared stories about our marriages and he told me he was separated from his wife, with whom he had been married for many years, and that his marriage had ended because of infidelity. He had hurt her very badly and felt he was just not suited for a serious relationship at that time.

I wasn't comfortable with the fact that he had cheated on his wife, although I believed he did feel genuinely remorseful over it. I remembered the times I had spent in a relationship where neither party had nurtured or prioritised the other and how powerless and angry I had felt. I also knew from when I was younger what it was like to be attracted to another man while in a relationship and feel unable to let go of either, so part of me understood that maybe Michael's situation was not as cut and dried as it appeared.

I realised just four weeks later that I did feel a strong connection with Michael, and I felt his attraction towards me. I was married, and Michael had made it clear he wasn't ready for anything other than a superficial relationship like the one he was having with his girlfriend. Whatever my feelings, our friendship needed to remain just that.

I did need to be honest about how I felt, though, even if it meant just letting him know and leaving it at that. I arranged to meet Michael at the Ballina Head Lookout. It was a beautiful warm evening in January around 9 pm after a meditation class. There were others sitting around looking out into the blackness of the sea while listening to the waves crash on the beach below. As I built up the courage to speak, we sat staring out over the water and talked about the earlier meditation class.

I had never been brave in affairs of the heart. My fear of rejection and lack of self-esteem have always made me hesitate to make any kind of first move, never mind openly pursue another, but on this balmy summer evening it wasn't the fear of rejection that made me hesitate. I had to know how Michael was feeling and, even though it could be seen as a risk, deep down I knew he cared enough about me to not make me feel ashamed or stupid to have asked the question.

'We need to talk about what's going on between us,' I said quietly. He nodded, never taking his eyes off the ocean below.

'Nothing is going on between us because you are married and I am, well, I am in a relationship with someone else,' he replied. 'We're friends. That's all it can be.' I nodded, as it was the answer I had expected and the only answer he could give, but I was disappointed. We continued to talk long into the night, our friendship still secure, but I felt a deep empty longing. At least now I knew: I loved him, but he didn't love me.

The next day Michael visited the shop, as he so often did, but things had changed. We were awkward, and I knew our relationship had shifted: that even a friendship with this man may not be possible. I was heartsick and embarrassed, but I also knew that I had not been imagining it. He had made me think there was something there too, and now I felt confused as though he had led me to feel something only to make me feel stupid and tricked into feeling something for him he had pretended to return.

'It's fine,' I said when he asked me what was upsetting me. 'I just have to come to terms with the fact that what I am feeling is nothing, just leftovers from our past-life connection. It's not anything for you as you are now. I just got it wrong.' He didn't say anything to that, but I sensed that he felt my words in a profound way as he left the shop. I thought that maybe that was it, that I would never see him again or maybe not again in this life anyway.

I decided I needed to get a healing to sort out my feelings, and booked a session with a friend who was an amazing Aboriginal crystal healer. As she worked through my chakras and helped me process my grief energy, she said that she didn't think that was the end for Michael and me. 'Everyone sees it, Mel, the connection between you,' she said, directing her energy into my throat chakra. 'Remember, he's only just learning about all this stuff. You have a lot more understanding about what is going on than he does. But don't worry, he will get there.'

I honestly didn't know if that was good news or bad. I had accepted that Michael didn't care for me and that was hard, but if he did and wouldn't tell me, wasn't that even harder?

As I walked out of the healing session a text alert on my phone sounded. I picked up my phone and saw a message from Michael: 'Hello, my favourite witch,' it read. 'Maybe you didn't get it so wrong. Call me.' Confused by the message, I called Michael and asked him, 'What are you talking about?'

There was silence for a moment and then he said, 'It means this feels an awful lot like love. I am in love with you.'

I didn't respond with a romantic swoon or a joyful declaration that I loved him too. What I said was: 'Oh, shit.' As much as I wanted this, the reality of it meant that everything was going to change. I knew I was going to leave my husband and I knew I was going to start a new life with Michael, and the enormity of it was almost overwhelming.

31. TRUST IN THE CONNECTION

You give me the kind of feelings
people write novels about.

– UNKNOWN

Michael was clear that any decisions I made needed to be thoroughly considered. I had my marriage and children to think about, and he took that as seriously as I did. He also made rules around what our relationship would look like till decisions were made, which included no physical contact of any kind: of any kind! I was not so adamant that a no-sex rule was the way to go. After all, what if I left my old life behind only to find out Michael was crap in bed, terrible at kissing or not the person I thought he was, or, or, or?

'You have to trust the soul connection,' Michael responded when I voiced my concerns. He was right. For our relationship to thrive it had to begin on solid ground without deceit or cheating on the other people in our lives. There was no getting around the fact that others were going to be hurt by our decision to have a life together, but that didn't mean we had to make it any worse than it needed to be. We would start our life together in the same way we wanted to continue it, and this meant no cheating.

Two days later I told Allen I had fallen in love with Michael and was ending our marriage. He knew he couldn't stop me from leaving, but he demanded to keep our girls with him. Above all else, I was determined not to drag my girls through a custody battle like I had experienced as a child. If this meant not being able to have them, well, that would be a consequence of my decision to end the marriage. I agreed to live at the shop while Allen and the girls stayed in our house, at least until we had everything sorted out.

Michael was a cotton farmer but ended up in Ballina as a result of his infidelity and the drought. Both had slammed him, and he came

173

to the coast to live with his daughter and heal his body, heart and self-esteem. It was time to get back to work, but cotton farming was no longer an option and he decided his path to making good money was by finding a job in mining. This meant he had to leave Ballina, at least for a while, as he went in search of work. Some of my friends and family took this as an opportunity to question Michael's commitment to me, seeing it as him leaving me to deal with the mess our relationship had created, but I knew it was the universe giving me the quiet and space I needed to ensure that I was making the right decision.

We had a few short days together before he left, and we spent it . . . holding hands! It sounds silly, but it's amazing how sensual just holding hands can be and how starting from basics means you savour what you have and appreciate each new step that follows. We also shared our first-ever kiss. It seemed I had waited forever for that kiss. As I melted into Michael's embrace it felt as though every one of those painstaking seconds I had waited till now had been worth it.

'I knew you had to kiss me eventually,' I said, laughing as we finally pulled away from each other. He laughed too, and two days later he was gone. I was once again on my own.

The next few weeks without Michael were hell as I adjusted to my new life living in the store and trying to prepare for Michael's eventual return. He was supposed to be gone for months but he returned after just two weeks, his efforts at finding a mining job having been spectacularly unsuccessful. We fell into each other's arms, totally and completely together for the first time. The no-sex rule no longer applied, and we took every advantage!

Our relationship was satisfying on so many other levels as well. I had never dared to dream that love could be so ultimately fulfilling. At night we walked on the beach or laid in bed talking for hours and making love for just as long. Over the following months I learned that Michael and I had shared at least seven past lives, but in each and every one we seemed unable to cement our relationship. It was never that we didn't love each other enough, just that we couldn't get our timing right as other things or other people kept coming between us. Both of us were determined that was not going to happen to us this time.

Michael still did not have a job and the earnings from the store were hardly enough to keep it afloat, never mind cover living expenses for the two of us. Michael and I were very independent people, and it was just a matter of time before he got a job as a fly-in fly-out (FIFO) pipe liner more than 4,000 kilometres away, in Western Australia.

I hated the thought of Michael being so far away for weeks at a time, as this had been the curse of our past lives and kept us separated even though we so badly wanted to be together. I worried endlessly that he wouldn't return during his layoff periods and would abandon me, but he didn't. On every break he came home, although the constant worry took a toll on our relationship and my mental health. The truth was that being with Michael was all-consuming; there were times when just looking into the depths of each other's eyes could bring us both to tears. Family and friends said this intensity wouldn't last forever and at the time we argued that they didn't know what they were talking about, because if they had the fortune of loving like we did they would know this intensity was limitless.

In hindsight I know they were right, and that the kind of intensity we had ends up becoming depleting no matter how much you love your partner. Loving Michael took everything from me, and I was willing to give. I started finding it hard to separate our past unsuccessful incarnations with our current reality, and there were times I even thought about ending my life.

Once again, a friend saved me. This time I confided my thoughts to end it all with my dear friend Jen, who worked with me part time in the store. She immediately booked an appointment with a psychologist, who patiently listened to me while I explained that I no longer wanted to live because Michael was leaving me yet again, the same as he had 500 years ago. It seemed I was destined to be in relationships where men left me, came back and then left me again. I just couldn't deal with it any longer.

The psychologist didn't even blink at my bizarre tales of past lives and soul connections; she just listened and let me work through my fears without judgement. She was simply amazing. Michael, too, was incredibly patient during this period, gently reminding me that we have to live in this life as it plays out but that it was going to be different from the ones before.

'I love you and you love me,' he told me. 'This job is what I need to do to heal myself; it's not about being away from you. I need to have the dirt in my hands, to let the land heal me so I can be the best I can for both of us. For now, you have to trust. Trust me, and trust that spirit has brought us together.'

I tried to, I really did, but it was so hard.

I was living alone in one of the treatment rooms I had converted into a bedroom. My only company was a black cat, Alchemy, who like any good witch's familiar was completely unpredictable. I had thought it a good idea to get a cat, because every witch needs a familiar and there is nothing so traditional as a black feline, but instead of being my companion and comfort Alchemy was my tormentor.

He was incredibly domineering, and took delight in terrorising me and anyone else who came into my shop. At night he insisted on sleeping curled on top of my face or perched on my head. It didn't matter how often or with how much force I pushed him off, he simply shook himself and made his way back to my head or face and settled down. Alchemy was relentless! His other favourite trick was to hide in a high place where he couldn't be seen, then pounce on me as I walked beneath him. His razor-sharp claws raked down my back or arm as he slid down onto the floor and then rushed away, a black flash too fast for me to ever catch and discipline.

He couldn't be trusted around any of the customers and often, particularly during meditation sessions, he found himself locked up in one of the unused therapy rooms. He hated it, and retaliated by completely destroying whatever was lying around.

Eventually I realised Alchemy would cause less damage if I allowed him to roam where he pleased and simply warned anyone in the sessions not to bother him. As soon as he realised he was no longer to be confined he happily pattered into the meditation session I was holding and then, surprisingly, sat quietly on my lap purring loudly. It was so unlike him I almost lost my concentration in the session, but then I realised he was not just in the room but had somehow managed to get into my meditative state as well.

In this particular meditation I was travelling back in time to the lands of ancient Egypt and there he was, this black cat of mine, only larger and sleeker, almost the size of a great black panther. In the meditation he acted not as my tormentor, but as protector and friend. We communicated without the use of spoken words and I realised that Alchemy had been my spirit animal all along, frustrated by my inability to connect with him.

Upon the completion of our meditation the rest of the group commented on how quiet Alchemy had been and how calm and contented he still seemed to be. It was like the horrible imp that I had shared my life and shop with had disappeared and a loving, calm kitten had stepped in to take his place. From that moment onwards Alchemy's terrorising behaviour ceased and he became a gentle and beloved companion. I think all of his previous bad behaviour had been his attempts to communicate with me, and now that that he had and I understood who and what he really was he was able to relax and no longer act out in frustration and annoyance.

Alchemy may have found a way to communicate and make peace with me but the same was not true in my relationship with Allen, which had gone from bad to worse as my relationship with Michael deepened. Allen felt as though he was stuck in a small town away from family and friends and everything he had ever known. It was true that he had moved to Ballina to save our marriage, and as far as he was concerned I had chosen to destroy it. I didn't remind him that it was his intimate connection with another woman that had been the mortal blow to our relationship, that all I had done was finally put us all out of our misery.

The girls were aged 12, 10 and seven and were managing the separation between Allen and I relatively well. I saw them as regularly as I could, going to their house at around 6.30 am to get them ready for school and drop them off on my way to work. I often reflected on those times and wondered if the girls were really okay, or whether I just wanted to believe they were so I didn't have to deal with the guilt.

I never really worried about Allen despite his claims of being heartbroken. I didn't quite believe he was as lost as he claimed, and six weeks after the official end of our union he began a new relationship with a woman whom he subsequently married. I'm not making any judgements about this and I'm glad he found someone else to love, because that's what I hope for him.

Ironically, it was me who felt alone and sad leading up to the divorce. Michael was still coming and going with his FIFO job and the children were living with Allen. I prepared to go to court and front up to the divorce proceedings alone and I didn't like it one bit, but fate is often kind to me and as luck would have it our small town had just one visiting magistrate, who came into town once a month. I thus found myself having the same divorce date as two of my dear friends. We decided to turn it into a mini celebration and met up for breakfast before heading off to court together. I wasn't alone after all.

The day after the court ruling the three of us threw a divorce party at the local pub. I admit I had more than a few drinks, which is very unlike me, but I had a lot to celebrate. I was officially divorced and free to be with my soulmate, and things were starting to look like they were working out.

32. MY TRUE PATH

We do not have a fear of the unknown.
What we fear is giving up the known.

– ANTHONY DE MELLO

During the first six months together with Michael I often brought the conversation around to the topic of marriage. I was divorced, but Michael was still legally married. I struggled with this, not because I was jealous but because in our past lives we had never made a commitment of marriage to each other, and this time had to be different. I didn't want to repeat the mistakes and tragic outcomes that seemed to have followed us through our past lives.

Michael felt that a piece of paper did not represent his commitment to me. 'Having a piece of paper with someone else doesn't represent a commitment to me either,' I argued back. He paused and we hugged, and he told me he loved me, but we remained unmarried.

I knew Michael loved me even when we were fighting. I never doubted it, yet his refusal to make our commitment formal made me feel as though I wasn't good enough. I now know that was because of my earlier relationships when I was so easily abused, discarded and disrespected, and because of the betrayal I felt over Allen's emotional friendship. Deep down the young, insecure girl who had allowed herself to believe she was not good enough for anyone still lurked, subconsciously feeding my insecurities and sense of inadequacy.

I could hear myself in my arguments with Michael sounding like that young petulant teenager, my fear and sense of worthlessness motivating me to keep pushing even though I knew he wasn't comfortable with how insistent I was being. After a while his discomfort became so clear that I couldn't help but see how my continued nagging about this was not rectifying the situation. Michael believed what he believed and

I believed what I did, and if I kept putting unnecessary pressure on what was in all ways that truly mattered a pretty great relationship, I might end up creating the outcome I was trying to avoid. I might be the thing that ruined this.

I decided to stop initiating marriage conversations and allow the relationship to develop at its own pace and in its own way. I would wait 12 months and see whether over that time I could become comfortable with living in the relationship I had, rather than try to constantly change it to reflect what I thought it should be. If I found after that time that I still felt the same way, and if Michael still insisted that he didn't need to get a divorce, then I would make a decision about whether or not to continue in the relationship. We found a semblance of peace, but even as I stuck to my word and never brought up the idea of marriage over all those months I never shook the feeling of not being good enough to marry.

As I dealt with my own trauma and history I was unable at first to understand why Michael was so resistant to divorcing his wife, but over time I began to understand that this was similar to Michael's initial fear of commitment when I first met him. Both responses were a product of his separation and hurt during that process, and although he and his ex-wife maintained an excellent relationship the fact that something you poured your heart and soul into did not turn out as you planned can have lasting emotional effects. Mental health can be challenging for everyone, and both men and women suffer from the effects when they are forced to deal with difficulty and emotionally challenging situations.

While I saw Michael as a resilient and fairly laid-back man, I also had to recognise that he had some challenges with depression. I started to see that Michael had two main gears: fun, carefree and fearless, like when he was riding his motorbike down the freeway well over the speed limit, and a slow, steady decline as he started to lose his enthusiasm for life and became depressed. Usually he would focus on some issue at work or home as the cause of his depression, but while things can be stressful, the problem with focusing on outside causes is that there are always events in life that cause stress and there will always be another issue.

Depression, sadness and emotional challenges are part of life. It's how we deal with it that defines how much those things affect us. Losing a relationship, like losing a person, can cause a state of grief, something that was not then properly considered when addressing the challenges of mental health in this country. Michael was going through the grief of losing his marriage, and even though he loved me he also had to process the loss he was experiencing through the separation with his ex-wife. He was suffering from the knowledge and guilt that he was to blame for hurting her and his children and the sense of loss over the life he had with them. It wasn't that he wanted them to go back to the way they had been, and in fact his ex-wife was unexpectedly incredibly generous and welcoming towards me as Michael and I built our relationship. However, grief still had to be processed, and we are generally very poor at doing so effectively.

The *Diagnostic and Statistical Manual of Mental Disorders* (more commonly known as the *DSM*), which is used by doctors to help diagnose and treat mental health issues, has started to acknowledge types of grief and how they can impact those experiencing it. According to the latest edition there are now three recognised types of grief: uncomplicated, complicated and prolonged. The first is the normal reaction to the loss of a loved one or a situation that had meaning; it is uncomfortable but usually requires just time and self-care to overcome. The latter two are more complex, as they acknowledge that in some cases of loss there can be additional complicated feelings of shame, guilt, anger and a loss of the sense of self. It was this that Michael was dealing with, and why he was so reluctant to completely sever his marital bond with his ex-wife even though he genuinely wanted to be with me.

I was also starting to get stressed about things. The store was wonderful for my spiritual growth but it had been a financial disaster. I needed to get out, but there were few opportunities to sell and I feared I would be saddled with the costs of it forever. Out of the blue, a former customer made me an interesting offer. She wanted to take over the store, so we came upon a clever solution: we swapped. I took over the lease of her house in Ballina and she took on the store. Once again, the universe had sorted out my problems.

Not only did this solve my financial issues, but living in the store had been difficult for me. The space was small and cramped and I had no privacy from staff or customers, who treated my private rooms like any other area of the shop. Now I could move into a house with room to have the girls stay with me when they chose, and almost without having a conversation about it Michael and I moved in together and set up our very first home together. It felt like we were beginning again, even though he still refused to formally end his marriage.

It wasn't a big house, but it was snug and cosy with room for additional guests if we wanted to host them. Michael's two children Jess and Daniel were living independently before Michael and I began our relationship so we really didn't need to worry about them, but my girls were still children and I wanted to ensure they felt their mother had not abandoned them. Michael and I agreed that we would never place any pressure on them, but if they ever wanted to they would always have a home with us.

Cassie-lee was the first of my girls to take up our offer, moving in with us just a few weeks after we set up after having an argument with her dad and his new partner. I knew she was angry with him and wanted me to side with her, but there was only one absolutely non-negotiable rule in my house: no matter what I would never say anything bad or demeaning about the girls' dad in front of them. Even when they were upset or angry with him I didn't join in or egg them on. Their relationship with their dad was important, and I would not be the one to ruin it. Even though it was tempting to fuel Cassie-lee's annoyance with her father, I simply let it go and welcomed her into our home without a word.

Cassie-lee had just turned 13 when she chose to live with us, and for a while I thought she would be the only one to move in. Then Allen and his new wife moved into a smaller house and there was no room for the other girls, so they also came to live with Michael and me. Allen and his wife happily accommodated the girls in their new home, but Teniel preferred to stay with us. My youngest daughter Jenna experimented with living between the two houses for a while, but she eventually decided it was just too hard living out of a suitcase and moved in.

The girls still saw their father and their relationship with Allen was quite good, but I think they just preferred the atmosphere in our house. I had a lot less rules than Allen did, as I trusted that giving the girls age-appropriate freedom and decision-making would give them the skills to manage situations better as they grew older. I also knew it could be hard to adjust to life with a new stepmum, and although I had nothing bad to say about Allen's new wife I understood why the girls preferred to stay with me. I was their mum, and they knew me.

Michael and I quickly found ourselves in a very small house with three kids, two dogs and Alchemy the cat. It was squishy, but we were a family and we managed.

I felt like my time at Magickal Realm had been an important step on my journey, but I still had not found my true path. I had developed my understanding of the spirit world and started to investigate my own abilities and of course I had met Michael, but it seemed like that time was at an end and something was pulling me back to where I had begun: working with people. I knew I had to do something meaningful, something that helped people, and Michael's experiences of depression were reminding me of my skills in counselling and community outreach.

As I watched Michael coping with his depression I understood many of the things I had seen while working in Aboriginal communities as a child protection officer. I realised many of the problems in our communities were symptoms of a profound and intergenerational grief that had never been properly healed or acknowledged.

Aboriginal communities can suffer from grief as they try to come to terms not only with their history and the loss of their culture, but also with the fact that they have survived when others did not. This can manifest as anger towards white culture or a rejection of their own Aboriginality, or in some terrible cases in self-medication and harm through the taking of drugs and alcohol or violence towards others in their community.

I have seen these things play out so tragically both within Aboriginal communities where I have worked and within my extended family. I have also seen the wasted lives of people who stay within the safety of their depression and how it destroys the soul of the person and affects anyone who tries to hold out their hand to help. Families, friends and loved ones are all affected and want to assist, but you can only put your hand out so many times before becoming at risk of being pulled down into someone else's depths of despair. That's the hard decision for those who love people who are struggling with mental illness: do you help, or do you watch?

I remember how helplessly my own family watched as I kept returning to toxic relationships and difficult situations, how my mother struggled with the loss of her children and how my father, sister and extended family struggled to move on after traumas, disappointments, relationship breakdowns and betrayals of trust. If there had been someone to help, could those things have been avoided or handled more effectively?

There is only so much that loved ones and family can do as they try to maintain a connection with someone who is falling into depths of sadness, depression and grief. My experiences, history and skills and training could be used in ways I had not realised before to help my community. That was when I decided I wanted to go back into the community and find ways to help those who were struggling – not as a child protection worker or a government official but as part of the community itself, helping those who needed it with counselling, support and training.

33. COMMUNITY

Family are the people we choose, not
always the ones we are born into.

– UNKNOWN

Over the next few years I started to develop my pathway back to the community, and I **soon** discovered **that my expertise and knowledge were highly valued** on committees and Aboriginal reference groups. **I found myself again being drawn to helping women and girls and was offered a job as a domestic violence court officer, supporting women through the court process of protecting themselves and their children from family violence.** A big part of this role was listening to the stories of these women, acknowledging and validating their fears and concerns while giving them the support they needed to move forward and get beyond their past. As I spoke to the women I found that I was an effective and empathetic counsellor.

Then, as now, funding and support for Aboriginal services came nowhere near covering the demand, and I found that I had to take on a lot of different part-time and temporary positions to stay in the communities, often providing services only as long as state or federal funding was available and finding that the money too quickly ran out.

The importance of government support for the Aboriginal welfare sector was a huge concern for me, and when I was offered an appointment as one of the Aboriginal representatives on the New South Wales Premier's Council for Women, reporting directly to then premier the Hon. Kristina Keneally, I jumped at the chance. Although it was only a temporary appointment for two years, I believed it would give me an opportunity to represent the views of New South Wales Aboriginal women and children at a state level. In some ways it was effective, but like so many government initiatives there was little beyond the press release and the declaration of 'listening to indigenous voices'.

Throughout my time on the council I was continually frustrated at the lack of progress or attention the council truly offered women, particularly those of Aboriginal descent. By the time the appointment came to an end I was somewhat disillusioned, and more convinced than ever that if we wanted real change for Aboriginal communities then we needed to engage directly with the people and create grass-roots and more trauma-based services.

With this in mind I took up a part-time community development role for a large counselling organisation, and through this made sure there were specific programs that allowed women the opportunity to be themselves. It was all about nurture, self-care and developing their own paths while providing a place where their voices could be heard. I started a weekly yarning and well-being group for Aboriginal women in my area and was given the freedom to run it any way the group decided was appropriate. We decided that drop-in, casual but supportive practical craft sessions were the way to go.

We called the group 'Goagan Dubay', which means 'beautiful women' in Bundjalung language, and it was made up of anywhere from eight to 12 ladies each week. We were all very spiritual and did some incredible work together. Sometimes we went out into the bush and created our own unique Aboriginal ceremony, and at other times we sat around talking about how our week had been and sometimes we did art together.

Alinta, the daughter of one of the original group members, became part of our group as we expanded. We older women loved it that the group had been graced by someone still in their teen years yet so in tune with the spiritual topics we talked about. She came from good stock, as her mum Dee was equally as amazing.

Alinta and Dee became part of the beautiful women family, who shared their loves, hopes, fears and life experiences with each other. It was a truly delightful space, so it was not surprising that Alinta chose a quiet yarning session to share the news that she was pregnant.

Despite her youth, everyone was convinced she would be an amazing mother and there was much celebrating and congratulations as a beaming Dee looked on proudly.

The father of Alinta's child was literally the boy next door: he lived in the house next to Alinta and Dee's with his mother, who seemed a little disapproving of the relationship between Alinta and her son. Nevertheless, he was a decent fella and he had promised to stick by Alinta as the two young people raised their child together.

Throughout her pregnancy Alinta shared her journey to motherhood with the group, gaining valuable advice, support and love from the older women, who considered themselves extended family to the beautiful young teenager. We were all extremely excited when the day of the birth arrived and I anxiously awaited news from Dee as to how things had gone for Alinta. Thankfully the birth was unremarkable, and a new baby boy was brought into the world and placed into Alinta's eager arms.

I met with Alinta's mother Dee a few days later for a coffee to see photos from the delivery room. As Dee proudly showed off the newborn grandchild her phone rang. She recognised the number and answered it frowning. 'What is it, bub?' she asked. I heard Alinta's voice on the other end: she was crying and hysterical. It was hard for Dee or me to make any sense out of what she was saying. 'Slow down, bub,' Dee said patiently. 'What's happened?'

Alinta took a few deep breaths, and although she was sobbing and her voice was shaky she managed to explain why she was so distressed. She told her mother she'd been exhausted and asked the dad to look after their baby for a few hours while she had a nap. Alinta had gratefully handed over the child and gone to sleep. When she awoke and went next door to collect her son, the baby's grandmother wouldn't let her in. Alinta was told that the baby would be staying with them.

At this, she related to Dee, Alinta became hysterical, demanding that her child be given back to her, and the police were called.

Child protection officers quickly arrived on scene, and in a jaw-dropping act of stupidity determined that the distressed teenage girl was abusive and violent and as a result the child could not be placed back in her care. They determined that the father was the best carer for a baby just a few days old and immediately handed him temporary custody of the child, warning Alinta that if she did not calm down and go back to her home she would be arrested. That was the beginning of the end of Alinta's life.

Alinta had been deemed an unfit mother based on no more than her Aboriginality and age.

Separated from her child by bureaucratic red tape and a flimsy shared fence line, Alinta became increasingly agitated. Frustrated and angered by the unfairness of the whole system, she started to fall into a deep, dark and dangerous depression that leeched all the hope and sunshine out of this previously joyful, bright young girl. Even so she fought on, doing everything she could to try to convince child services that she was not and could never be a threat to her own child.

After eighteen months, the grandmother and father were granted a protective order against Alinta that dictated she could not go within 100 metres of them or her child. Alinta still lived next door, so this order had the effect of forcing her to move out of her mother's home and into an isolated flat a few streets away where she sat alone and desolate, unable to wake up from the nightmare that was unfolding all around her.

Alinta tried to fight it, facing each day like a warrior, but her depression was becoming insurmountable. The inability of anyone in the system to listen to her side or have empathy for a young mother whose baby has been ripped out of her hands became overwhelming, and a few days before her 21st birthday she was unable to fight it any longer. That evening Dee found her daughter hanging from the exterior clothesline. She had taken her own life. The system Alinta had courageously fought against for more than 18 months, a system that was supposed to protect the most vulnerable, had finally and fatally defeated her.

No one can know exactly what Alinta was thinking as she made that fateful decision, lonely and distraught and away from her child. There is no doubt that the actions of the child protection services were to blame for her feelings of hopelessness and loss.

As Dee held her daughter's lifeless body she vowed to fight the system that had taken her daughter. That night, in the deepest despair, she rang the local child protection office to accuse them of being the reason for her daughter's suicide. Any empathetic, understanding human would have realised that a grieving mother lashing out at the horror of her child's unnecessary death should have been treated with care and consideration. Instead, after listening to the message that had been left the night before the workers of that office deemed Dee's words to be a credible threat to themselves and Dee's grandchild and issued a new protective order that prevented Dee from seeing her grandchild.

I was consumed by grief at Alinta's death, and guilt that I couldn't have done more for her. I had tried everything I could think of, but it had not made any difference. Even with my knowledge and experience of the system I had failed to find a way for Alinta to survive it. As I felt the anger, bewilderment and frustration build I also felt something else, a presence all around me during my grief, and I heard Alinta speak as loud and clear as I ever had while she had been alive. 'Make it count, Mel,' she said in her soft, beautiful voice. 'Make my voice count.' I nodded and wiped the tears angrily from my eyes. She wanted me to make her life and death meaningful, to use it to help others in similar situations and I was going to do so. The only question was how.

Truth finds a way: that is what I believe, and it is a fundamental pillar of Aboriginal cultural ideals. Truth telling is an important aspect of coming to terms with what has happened. The act of speaking, of shedding light on injustice, is a way to make injustice less overwhelming and perhaps the first step in overcoming it. Someone always listens as long as truth continues to be spoken.

We decided to make a small documentary about Alinta. In the documentary we told her story, and *Learning from Alinta* was released online with funding from a mental health organisation based in Melbourne called Beyond Blue. Thanks to them and the tireless efforts of many within the Aboriginal communities, who helped spread word about it, we managed to get Alinta's story out there.

It felt good to tell the story. I had come into this community as someone who wanted to help, someone who wanted to give some support, structure and assistance to the women here. I realised, though, that there was only so much I could do in temporary roles as a consultant or advising on forums. They mattered in the abstract, in working on the wider issues for Aboriginal women and girls, but if I wanted to make a real, fundamental, practical difference then something else was needed. Aboriginal people needed a full-time advocate, someone who could work with them at a grass-roots level to navigate the system: not as an outsider or protection worker but as someone who could mediate between the two and get real results. Who better to do this than me?

34. BACK TO SCHOOL

Anyone can get a degree or a certificate in something. Big deal. A piece of paper from a university somewhere doesn't define a person. It won't tell you who I am.

– RACHEL GIBSON

I may have had years of experience and an unrivalled understanding of the child protection system as it related to Aboriginal people, but I didn't hold any formal qualifications. I knew that without them I would not be taken seriously; hadn't my efforts with the child protection services in Alinta's case shown that ever so clearly?

This was not a new problem, and it was one I shared with many Aboriginal people. The education system can be difficult, out of touch or just plain inaccessible to Aboriginal people, particularly women, and my background had certainly given me scant opportunity to pursue higher education. I had to work to put a roof over my head and provide for my family and didn't have the time or resources to take on a full-time university course. I had attended a forum as a delegate in 2008 where the main topic was a discussion of the issues around Aboriginal employment and the lack of opportunity for our people to gain professional positions. Like me, I encountered a lot of other Aboriginal women there who had amazing skills but lacked the qualifications and often the confidence to apply for such jobs.

I believed then and still believe now that experience is often more relevant than a degree particularly in social work or the welfare sector where the skills of doing the job are rarely attained through reading books and attending lectures. Aside from that, the costs of getting

191

such a degree were exorbitant. Why, I thought, should I waste time and money to get a piece of paper to prove that I can do something I am already doing extremely well?

As I thought about the problems I wondered if I was using this as an excuse not to further my education. Was I just scared that I wasn't smart enough? I only had a Year 10 certificate, no other educational background, but would my experience make up for that? Could I get accepted into a degree program? I decided the only way to find out was to try, and as it turned out my experience and knowledge were seen to be valuable after all: in 2008 Southern Cross University in Lismore offered me a place in their master's degree in Aboriginal Healing and Trauma.

Suddenly any excuse was gone, and I decided if I really wanted to make a difference for people like Alinta and other Aboriginal mothers and children I would be stupid not to take this opportunity. I swallowed my reservations and enrolled in the degree.

On the first day of the course they threw us into the deep end. We were tasked with undertaking a mock counselling session with one of the other students as a way of evaluating our listening and counselling skills. I felt quite confident as these were skills I used every day in my professional counselling role, a role that required I be assessed twice yearly by practice experts in order to maintain my position. The mock counselling session was simple in comparison and I happily sat down across from fellow student Harriet as she told me about some problems she was having at home.

I listened carefully and we engaged for 15 minutes going through concerns as I helped guide her through the process of considering her options. At the end of the session Harriet was impressed with the process and thanked me profusely. I was pleased to have helped and pleased that I was doing so well on my very first day. Maybe this academic stuff was not so hard after all.

However I was upset to be told in front of other students that I was moving into skills I wasn't ready for. Confronting the lecturer after this incident gave me an opportunity to understand how much braver I am than I realised and that I can stand up to people in authority rather than my old reaction of dissolving into tears. When the lecturer apologised I accepted the apology and moved away, feeling the strongest I had for years.

A month or so after that I was asked by the students' association if I could act as the unofficial counsellor for the students in my course. Since our unit dealt primarily with trauma and healing it was not unusual for the content to trigger emotional concerns in the students themselves, and they often needed someone to chat things through with them. I don't know if the students who had witnessed my interaction with the lecturer that day were the ones who suggested to student services that I may be the most suitable person in the course for that particular role, but I suspect that could easily have been the case.

Overall, my time at university was a mixed bag. I did learn the fancy language and terminology for things I had been doing instinctively for years. I learned I have an eclectic counselling style, where I use a bit from here and there and add in some weird stuff of my own, and that this is a perfectly valid and valued approach that made me feel good about my personal style. In the end, when I walked out of the university with a master's degree I didn't think I had learned that much, but the paper gave me credibility and the letters I can put after my name now can open doors that were previously closed to me. It was what I needed, and what would be valuable as I developed my role as an Aboriginal advocate.

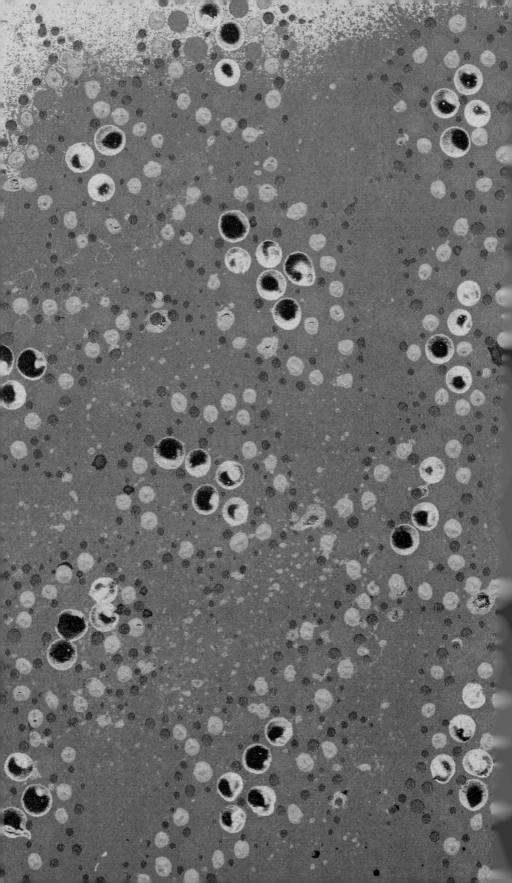

35. REWINDING TIME

Returning to where it once began.

– MEL BROWN

As Christmas approached I was juggling work and study and eagerly awaiting Michael's return from his FIFO job. He was travelling home for a few weeks' break, which was the most time we had spent together since February 2007. When I saw him arrive my heart filled with such love and excitement: I missed him so much when he was away and hated every moment he was gone.

This would be our first Christmas together, and I had put so much thought into making it special because I knew it needed to be memorable. We celebrated Christmas with my girls on Christmas Eve so they could be with their dad on Christmas Day. I have always felt strongly that special days can be celebrated any time, particularly if this reduces the stress for the kids having to choose between being with their mum or dad. It's something I still do some 18 years later.

I prefer to give gifts than to receive them. It's not that I don't appreciate the time and effort that goes into buying gifts; it's just that my love language is acts of service. Empty the dishwasher, vacuum the house, bind the folders I need for training next week – that's what makes me feel loved, and my outgoing love language is gift giving. I love to shop and buy gifts, so this Christmas was special because I had spent so much time deciding what to get Michael. As Christmas morning dawned I was excited to give Michael a camera he had been looking at for months.

With a gigantic grin on his face, Michael excitedly presented me with a huge box. I hadn't thought much about what Michael would buy me for our first Christmas together and was surprised by my disappointment as I began to open the present. I hadn't realised till then that I still held on to the hope that he would want to marry me, and that his Christmas present to me might be an engagement ring. Looking at this large box I knew it wasn't that. I started ripping off the paper and opening the cardboard lid off the box. Inside was another box, wrapped in more festive paper but of another colour. I gave Michael a slightly puzzled look but could see that he was grinning mischievously.

'You need to open that one too,' he said.

I did, and the smaller box inside that, and the smaller one inside that. As each box opened my expectation started to rise. The boxes were clearly diminishing in size, and I started to suspect that the final one would be small and square and contain a diamond engagement ring after all. Finally, he was going to marry me!

I came to what turned out to be the last box. It was not square but rectangular, about the size of a small manila envelope. My heart started to slowly sink as I unwrapped it and saw what was inside. There was nothing small and glittering, nothing made of diamonds or gold: just a bunch of travel brochures. I tried to hide my disappointment, but it must have shown on my face. How could it not? What the hell kind of present was this anyway, a bunch of booklets? I couldn't even understand what he was trying to give me as I was trying to sort the roller coaster of emotions I had just experienced in the space of the past minute. I was exhausted.

Michael sensed my confusion and took the brochures from my hand. 'We're going to England, Mel. You and me.' I looked at him, dumbfounded. England? Why would I want to go to England? 'So we can break the curse,' he explained.

My confusion cleared and any disappointment I had felt at the lack of a ring disappeared right along with it. Over the course of our relationship we had spoken many times about our past lives together. In each life that was revealed to us we had ended up separating or being separated, and this had created an underlying dread for me in this life, in this manifestation of our relationship. I was so sure we would be separated again, and the thought of it was unbearable.

We had completed several guided meditations to try to work out why each life we had lived had led to us being torn apart, but had never found anything close to an answer until we journeyed all the way back to one of our earliest lives together. In this incarnation we were in the England of the Middle Ages, living together on the cliffs by the sea. During our meditation I saw how happy I was, how together we felt, but Michael was taken from me by circumstance never to return. I was devastated but I was also a strong and practising wise woman, and in my grief I concocted a powerful spell that I cast into the ocean that cursed Michael for leaving me and ensured that my heart would never be broken like that again.

Spellwork and magic are powerful things and should never be used in times of distress or anger, as our emotional selves often do not honour the seriousness of what we do. So it was in this case as that magical spell flew out into the raging tides and was swept into the sea, carrying my intentions with it. In my emotional state my intention was not clear, and instead of ensuring Michael was mine I cast a curse that told the universe he could never truly, completely have me. It was this spell that had turned into the curse of our relationship. That damn threefold law was coming at me again as I foolishly acted in ways that created problems in our relationship when there didn't need to be. By casting that curse I had condemned all of our lives into a cycle of sabotage and mistrust, which had led to us never being able to be fully, completely together.

Michael had been thinking about this and had realised that until the curse was lifted we would remain in a state of uncertainty in our relationship. I would remain insecure of his love, my heart hardened against the possibility of heartbreak as I pushed and needled and tested his love for me over and over again. That is not good for any relationship and Michael wanted us to get beyond it, as did I.

It wasn't that easy, though, as the curse had been cast in the rugged coastline of England not far from the famed site of Tintagel Castle, the home of King Arthur's Camelot. It was so far away from our little house on the north-eastern coast of Australia, and to lift a curse you have to be at the place the curse was cast.

Michael had given me the best Christmas gift ever, the opportunity to change our past and our future and finally rid ourselves of the doubts and ill omens that had hung over our lives across lifetimes.

I threw my arms around him: this was exactly what we needed, and how clever it had been of him to have thought of it. We packed our bags and headed over to the ancient lands of Britain.

I was so excited on the plane I barely slept for the 27 hours of travel, although Michael seemed to have no trouble dropping off to sleep in the seat next to mine. I watched him, his huge, beautiful frame cramped into the economy-class seat and his legs sprawled over into my legroom as he dreamed of things to come. I wished I could be so peaceful and calm but, maybe, once the curse was lifted I could sleep just as well. We stepped onto British soil in the dark hours of the morning. It was quiet and peaceful, as though the entire place had been lying dormant and awaiting our arrival.

On our first day we went to visit the Tower of London, but as we crossed Tower Bridge towards the famed building a sense of dread and horror overcame me. I didn't have a clear picture of what had happened to me, but I knew that the tower was a place of strong psychic connection and I wasn't ready to re-experience whatever had occurred there in one of my previous lives.

Michael and I decided we would leave London as soon as possible, and within a day we were driving out into the beautiful English countryside. England is so green and lush, a complete contrast to the scrubby faded greens and vibrant yellows of our home in Australia, yet this felt like home. There is no other way to describe it: it just felt as though I had found the place where my soul belonged.

Michael had planned the trip in great detail, finding as many places as he could identify from our meditations and visions of our past lives together. It felt like rewinding time itself as we journeyed back into our pasts with each new place and each old life gifting us more and more knowledge about how we had come to be where we were. Our first stop was Greenham Hall in Somerset, a gorgeous country estate that had been built in the mid-1800s. It was like it had never met the modern era, with its great staircases heading upwards from each side of the oversized entry towards the period perfect guest rooms.

As I awoke the next morning in Michael's arms the memories of a past connected to this country came quickly, and like many times before it was hard to differentiate the present time from the past. I saw everything in intricate detail and smelt every smell as though it was right under my nose. The feelings were as real to me then as they had been previously.

I saw my Michael of the past standing on the riverbank we could see through the hall's master windows. He was watching me, his skin tanned and his arms and torso muscular through the clothes he wore, clothes of a 17th-century soldier. The scars on his hands and face told stories of battle, and there was an air of arrogance about him. He was a leader among men, yet no men followed him. His very presence commanded respect, and he was a man of wisdom and of war.

His most striking feature was his beautiful eyes, and even from a distance I could feel them looking into my soul, assessing me and deciding what to do. His eyes were battle weary, with no fight left in them – at least not for today, and not for me. These were the same eyes I knew so well in my current life. This was Michael as he had been hundreds of years ago. Destruction, chaos and violence lingered just below the surface, and I could almost see the internal struggle taking place inside this man. He was unable to decide whether he should destroy me or hold me. I knew I should have been scared, but this man was no stranger to me. My heart had already told me that I had loved this man before, just not in this lifetime.

In my vision I also saw myself, living among the small hills on the other side of the river. I was a healer of sorts. Villagers came to me when they were sick, and I treated them with herbal medicines. I kept my distance from the village and its folk, living by myself in a small cottage with dirt floors and a straw roof, a fireplace at one end and bed at the other. The cottage was basic, with a table and two stools in close proximity to the fireplace. In winter the cottage was shared with the animals to keep them warm and protected from the harsh cold outside. Life was hard, but I was happy. I was a single woman and my reclusiveness possibly kept me from answering to charges of witchcraft from jealous wives.

Michael returned often, not for healing but for companionship, and I never knew or asked anything of him: where he went and what he did while he was away. We didn't talk about what he did, but I never doubted I was the only woman in his life and that he would always protect me and return to me. I knew he would be with me whenever it was safe to do so and that the depth of his love for me could not be described with mere words. I remembered healing his wounds when he appeared, often late at night or early in the morning. I was his safe haven, the place he could return to be healed, loved and nurtured.

Even in his deepest sleep he would still be alert and responsive to the slightest sound that was out of place. Even in the present day when Michael sleeps he is ready to respond immediately to any change in sound or energy. I do now what I did back then: I gently place my hand on him to ground his energy, and quietly tell him everything is okay.

I remembered the homecomings and the departures. The homecomings were filled with so much joy but were always quickly replaced by fear and sadness that he would leave again. I recalled the agony of waiting for him, and of being in limbo while I impatiently awaited his return. It was exactly the way I felt in my current life each time Michael left and went back to work on the pipelines.

As I lay in Michael's arms in the present time at Greenham Hall I recounted the vision I had just seen and how similar it was to our current lives, and also how different. 'We keep living the same lives,' I said, 'but I can't lose you in this life. We need to change the story of you leaving and leaving and leaving again.'

Michael nodded. 'That's why we're here, Mel.' He pulled me closer and made love to me again.

We left Greenham Hall, uplifted and hopeful and headed to the place where it had all begun: the legendary site of Camelot. The place that is generally agreed to have been Arthur's magical kingdom of Camelot is a site called Tintagel. It's an extraordinary castle that perches on the edges of the English county of Cornwall and overlooks the sea and the world beyond. It is a ruin now accessible via a steep and rickety climb, but long ago it was the home not just of King Arthur and Merlin but of me and Michael as well, many lifetimes ago. It was there that I had created a curse to prevent Michael being able to stay with me anymore and cast it into the ocean.

Arriving at Tintagel was overwhelming enough, but getting up to the ruined castle seemed almost impossible. First we had to traverse down a steep cliff, then up again in a different direction before heading down a couple hundred steep stone steps carved into the cliff's side towards the water, then across a stone bridge to the outcrop where the castle once stood, then up several hundred more stone stairs before finally arriving at the castle ruins. It was exhausting, and even more exhausting to realise you had to do it all again on the return.

A huge bridge was built across to the castle in 2019, as the goat tracks and impossibly steep stairs we had had to navigate were no longer deemed safe enough to access the castle ruins, and I often think how much easier it would have been if we had waited a few years to make the pilgrimage, but I'm glad we didn't wait because we had waited long enough through many lifetimes. An easier journey was not worth the cost of the curse continuing for several more years, causing more worry and strife between us.

As I laboured up those endless stairs, my back and legs aching, I knew I was thoroughly exhausted. I didn't have the energy to continue,. I stopped in the shadow of the old gatehouse entry and turned to Michael and burst into tears. Even if I could get across I wouldn't have the energy to do what I needed to do. Michael pulled me close, looked deep into my eyes and said: 'You don't have to prove anything. You can do what you need to do from here.' He kissed me gently then walked away.

Suddenly I was alone, and I looked out into the ocean. The sound and fury of the waves crashing onto the rocks below seemed to somehow feed my soul, and some of my energy returned. I drew power from the earth, from the sea and from my own spirit and took myself back to that time and place hundreds of years ago when I had cursed us. I stood in that mist of time and space and forgave Michael. I forgave myself. I revoked the curse and repented for ever having cast it, then I silently chanted a new spell, bathed in light and hope and with full reverence for what I was doing, my intention clear and sparkling. I sent out the clear intention that Michael and I should have a relationship now that could grow beyond anything it had ever been in any of our past lives, creating for us a happily ever after.

As I finished Michael magically appeared beside me. He pulled me close again and kissed me. This is the man I never wanted to be parted from again, the man I wanted to be with for the rest of my life. Married or not I couldn't live without him, and I experienced my first realisation that maybe marriage wasn't that important. Being with Michael was everything. With this, I let go of a huge weight from my very being.

Reality soon came crashing back, though, and I groaned when I thought about the trek back into town, about that long walk up and down the goat tracks. However, as I turned around to start our dreaded journey back I stopped and laughed: I remembered a shortcut that was known to me from my earlier life living in that very spot. I led Michael to a stone wall covered in bushes, pushed them aside and climbed over the brick wall. Michael gave me a puzzled look, wondering what I was planning, but he followed me through and onto an overgrown goat track that led us back to town in a very short 20 minutes with hardly a hill to climb.

How did I know that track was there? I just did; it was a memory from my past. I had never been to England before, let alone to Tintagel, so even I had to marvel at the accuracy of my memory from a past life.

36. BREAKING THE CURSE

Forever is a measure of time used by
people who share an ordinary love. Our
extraordinary love is immeasurable
. . . for us, forever just won't do.

– STEVE MARABOLI

The following day everything seemed brighter, lighter and full of hope. We headed to Glastonbury, a spiritual touchstone in the southwest of England in the county of Somerset. It is famous for a music festival, but back in the Middle Ages Glastonbury hosted the portal to the mythic lands of Avalon and the lands of the faeries. It was the home of the Lady of the Lake, who gifted the magical sword Excalibur to Arthur and made him king. It was a sacred and magic place governed by women who used ritual and sacred rites to connect with the goddess.

To say I was excited was an understatement. Glastonbury had always been a magical place to me, and I recalled several experiences I had where connections with it had manifested in my current life. Perhaps the most amusing had happened in Magickal Realm when I was the owner. I was there dusting the shelves when a woman with an enormous regal energy strode into the store. As soon as she saw me she exclaimed: 'Oh, my god, it's you!' I had never met this woman before in my life and had no idea who she had mistaken me for. She must have noticed my confusion, for she hurried over and took my hand. 'It's me, Guinevere,' she said. 'Lancelot and Arthur are here too!'

Okay, I'm one for having an open mind to most things, but there was no one with her: no one I could see, anyway. Her next words to me were mixed with reverence and disbelief: 'You're the Lady of the Lake. Don't you remember our conversations, don't you remember us?'

Anyone else may have thought this woman was crazy, but I immediately knew she wasn't. You see, I had already had visions and past-life regressions where I had been made aware that I was indeed one of the ladies of the lake, a few generations prior to the Arthurian legend. I say 'ladies', because many people are not aware that there were nine ladies of the lake. They were the keepers of Excalibur before and during King Arthur's time. I had known for many years since embarking on my journey to self that I was the seventh Lady of the Lake. The best-known one, Morgaine or Morgan le Fay, who came two generations after me, was my granddaughter. Standing there looking at this woman, I did wonder if I was as crazy as her but I couldn't let this opportunity pass. I found us some privacy in a vacant therapy room and for the next hour we compared stories. Glastonbury featured in many of them.

I was finally seeing the place for myself in real time, and I was not disappointed: it had a magical feel and every second shop was either a goddess or witchcraft store! It was bright and cheerful and full of life, but there was also a solemness to the place that let the tone rise above the tourists and the commerce and made you feel as though you really were somewhere sacred. Michael encouraged me to have a tarot reading, laughing when I hesitated. 'Come on, Mel, how often are you going to have the chance to have your tarot cards read in the very heart of magic?'

Of course I had to agree, and I found a tarot reader whose energy seemed to work well with my own. 'Welcome back, my lady,' he humbly greeted me as he bowed his head in reverence. I smiled shyly and wondered if he greeted everyone like that. He continued, stating that I had returned home and that my task was to leave the past behind.

I was pleased by the accuracy, and nodded when he told me that my task had been achieved and I was free to move on with the future. He then mentioned a handfasting that was around me, and that I would live happily ever after. When he mentioned the handfasting I told the reader that was not accurate. I had released my need for a marriage just the day before, at Tintagel; he must be confusing it with that. He wasn't convinced and kept circling back to it, but I was adamant that he was incorrect. He moved on with the reading, giving so much specific and useful information that I forgave him the misstep of the handfasting image. Sometimes as readers we mix up messages or don't quite know exactly what the images symbolised, so I assumed that had been the case in this reading.

After the reading I met Michael at Glastonbury Abbey, the final resting place of King Arthur. It was a very emotional place for me because I was flooded by memories: not of King Arthur, as I didn't have specific memories of him there, but of later times when the English church started disrespecting the old religions and stole sacred sites for their new churches such as this very abbey.

From there we moved on to the Chalice Well, where legend said the sacred waters of the well were linked to the Holy Grail. Upon arriving we were told they were closed for the day, then a lovely elderly lady told us to go on in. As she had already counted the days takings we could go in for free.

Michael and I made our way directly to the top of the site, where the Chalice Well is located. We sat quietly for some time paying our respects. Michael left me alone and wandered off to explore the gardens, and I sat within the energy of the goddess and discreetly dropped a crystal into the well as an offering. I had chosen this particular crystal before leaving Australia and taken it along with me the previous day to Tintagel, so it felt right to leave it here in the waters of the goddess.

As I made my way down the Chalice Well gardens I found Michael at King Arthur's court and healing pool. The trickling water, which was no higher than a few metres above us, gently tumbled over the side of the waterfall, flowed between water-polished stones and gathered in the shallow pool a few feet below. Michael motioned for me to stand on the other side of the waterfall on one of the less slippery rocks as he stood opposite me, the thin stream of water following between us. He cupped his hand and collected the holy water, then gently trickled the water onto my forehead while looking deep into my eyes. He recited:

With this water I cleanse the past.
With the universe as our witness
In this time of the spring equinox
And the full moon, I heal our past.

I was so overcome with emotion I couldn't speak, but there was no need for me to say anything as Michael reached into his pocket and brought out a ring, and then slowly and deliberately asked me to marry him.

I had finally let go of the need to get married, so of course now he asked me to spend the rest of this life and any others with him! That is how the universe works: it gives you what you have worked for and rewards selflessness, not selfishness. It's not hard to guess my answer, although I was in such shock it possibly took a few seconds longer than Michael had been expecting for me to give it. Finally, I uttered the words of acceptance and Michael said: 'I now break the cycle.' He kissed me to seal our promise to each other, then he solemnly asked me to take off my shoes and we stepped into the healing pool.

It was freezing cold, but I don't remember feeling it as we stood together in that water, kissed again and pledged ourselves to each other, making a sacred commitment to our future together.

After we had put our shoes and socks back onto our slightly frostbitten toes we found a quaint old English pub across the road serving St Patrick's Day green beer and celebrated our engagement. It was so different from our other conversations about marriage: this time we were both excitedly talking wedding plans, with Michael insisting it must take place before the end of the year.

'But you're still married,' I said.

Michael shook his head. 'I filed for divorce on the day we left.' His intent had always been to marry me; he just wanted to make sure he did so after I had let go of our past. Michael and I were married on 12 December 2008, exactly two years after the day we had met. Despite outward appearances Michael has always been a romantic, and as I stood beside him at our wedding ceremony looking into his eyes and saying my vows, our children watching with tearful joy, I knew that the curse had truly been lifted and we would be together forever.

I may not have started out in life knowing how to find the right man, and the goddess and ancestors know that the universe gave me a lot of trials and tribulations along the way, but she definitely saved the best for last: I know Michael will be the one and last great love of my life. I have loved and still love this man more than I could have believed a heart and soul could love another, and I know there will never be anyone else in this life or the next for either of us.

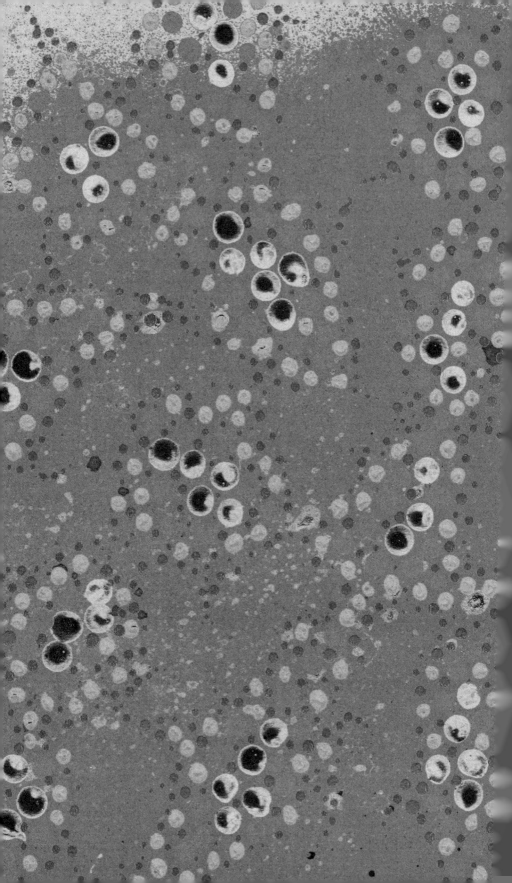

37. RETHINKING THE FUTURE

If you are creative, you get busier as you get older.

– Tony Bennett

My personal life was settled, my home was secure and life with Michael was good. I felt as though I was where the universe wanted me to be, but there was still something I needed to do. Around me I saw the challenges and disconnections that still existed between the welfare sector and Aboriginal communities, and I knew I could offer something important. I spent the next few years building my reputation as a cultural workplace trainer and consultant. I developed and delivered training to tens of thousands of people and consulted to government regarding specific cultural needs.

In 2016 the universe provided the means to take the next step on my Dreaming when I saw an advertisement for Aboriginal facilitators to undertake contract work to the New South Wales child protection service. The roles had been created as a way to provide mediation for Aboriginal people engaged in the child protection system.

I attended a training course in my first week and was appalled by how little the training or materials reflected the real needs in Aboriginal communities or had any understanding of the ways in which each community differed: not just in location but in attitude, outlook, customs and community organisation. If I had been younger I might have simply ignored these issues – after all, I had worked within flawed systems before – but I was wiser and stronger and I had a purpose in mind.

These services didn't need to just exist; they needed to work. Aboriginal people had been misrepresented and underserviced for too long. I remembered what had happened to Alinta, and how the available services had so abysmally failed to properly engage with her. What was needed was proper, effective training that reflected the reality of the job. The family group conferencing model was an opportunity to actively create genuine and significant change, but the training missed its mark.

'This training is not going to cut it,' I said to the person conducting the training. 'It isn't practical and it doesn't take in the real on-the-ground experiences of people working with this system.'

The trainer just smiled at me. 'This training program has been approved by the child protection department and has to be delivered as such,' they said. I read between the lines and acknowledged the trainer's responsibilities to deliver training content whether you believed it or not.

I quickly completed my qualification and, with a hint of arrogance but fuelled with commitment to my People, I arranged a meeting with the powers that be in New South Wales child protection. I boldly pitched the idea of writing a new training program that would use all of my experience and knowledge, all the lessons I had learned in my years working in community navigating child protection and being a counsellor. I was granted permission to create new family group conferencing training.

Having to now literally put my money where my mouth was, I set about writing a program that included lessons I had learned from the huge failures I had seen and the successes I had experienced while working with Aboriginal families. I'm still delivering this training many years later, and in my introduction to students I talk about how much I sincerely love the model and how it is the only practice I have seen that can make a real difference to families. The model acknowledges the family as being the experts in their own lives and recognises they have the ability to come up with their own plans to manage child protection concerns.

As a trainer and facilitator I continue to learn as much if not more than the participants, in environments where everyone's voice is shared and heard. I knew from experience that it was a rare day working in community when I didn't learn from the people I spoke to, and that true, real connections happened through conversations, yarns and chats and feeling safe to share stories.

Michael runs our business from home. We have any number of contractors working for us delivering services to the New South Wales Department of Communities and Justice, previously known as the Department of Family and Community Services, which oversees child protection, foster care and family support services across New South Wales. I am finally able to start changing the culture of these places at a grass-roots level, providing proper training and support that could hopefully help avoid the kinds of situations I had seen occurring in the past. Sometimes it's not easy, because as much as I was trying to change the conversation there were still real and profound issues with the very foundations of social services in this country, particularly for Aboriginal people.

One of the constant issues is what to do when children need to be put into care. The guidelines seem straightforward, but there is a lot of variation in the ways in which different regions and individuals interpret or enforce specific policies. In some areas there is a zero-tolerance policy for drug use in families where child protection services are involved, and the use of any substance no matter how minor can result in children being summarily taken into care. In other areas where there are simply not enough services or where drug and alcohol abuse is rife, the policy is less rigorous and a strategy of harm minimisation is employed.

Many child protection problems can be effectively solved by engaging with families rather than being adversarial or simply not listening. That doesn't happen enough, not because caseworkers are cruel or uncaring but because there is not the time or resources needed to undertake engagement with Aboriginal families or communities in a meaningful and understanding way. Most social services are underfunded, overburdened and under-resourced, leading to burned out or disillusioned staff who can't respond effectively to every case presented to them.

Most of the people who work within the social welfare sector, whether in government departments or with charities and not-for-profit organisations, are genuinely trying to do the right thing, but if they are not properly supported or adequately trained then negative outcomes will always arise. Add to that mix the times when the race, geographical location and economic situation of the people engaging with the system are viewed negatively, and you end up with wildly varied outcomes and no clear expectation that families will be treated with care and respect.

As I developed my business I noted that one of the greatest issues within the child protection space was the lack of foster carers. Since the mid-1990s the policy has been to try to place Aboriginal children within their family network or community with Aboriginal carers; however, there is a lack of training and resources given to Aboriginal communities to facilitate them to become formal, designated foster carers. While it is important that there is some kind of rigorous process to ensure that foster carers are safe and appropriate, in my opinion the current processes are poorly thought out and result in perfectly suitable families and carers failing to be approved based on elements that have little to do with their ability to care for a child and more to do with general biased assumptions about what a good foster carer looks like.

There is no easy fix for foster caring. Taking a child from their family and placing them in care will always be ethically, morally and practically difficult, but there are things we can do to make this less damaging to the children and families. A main part of our ever-expanding business is to assess carers to care for Aboriginal children. We are absolutely rigorous in our assessing process, but we are able to cast a cultural lens over our assessments to ensure carers are safe and culturally responsive to the children who may end up in their care.

An example of the work we do concerns a group of seven siblings that had been taken into care the previous month. As is so often the case, the children had been split up and farmed out to a variety of placements, most of them insecure and temporary. Not a single one had been placed with a family member. This would have remained the situation if an Aboriginal caseworker had not been allocated to the case and been appalled by the lack of effort that had been put into finding suitable family placements. How is it possible that not a single relative could be found who was willing to take those children on?

I was contracted to engage the family in an attempt to find family placement for the children. After two short weeks and more than 7,000 kilometres of travel by car and air I was able to find extended family that had never been approached to care for the children. Suddenly, the children had the opportunity to live with family and maintain familial connections rather than living disconnected from each other and their greater community. I was so pleased to have gained this outcome, but I knew it was only possible because someone within the child protection system cared enough to question the situation and look for alternatives. Without the placement of Aboriginal caseworkers or at least those with an understanding of the specific needs of Aboriginal families, poor decision-making will continue to happen within the child protection and social welfare sectors.

This is not to say that all Aboriginal communities are victimised or in need of welfare help. That is not the case, and a damaging narrative that is often spun is that Aboriginal communities are in need because they are unable to access the economic or structural resources to help themselves.

An Aboriginal community on one of the islands off the coast of Australia provides a particular case in point. They have a strong economy thanks to mining royalties, but there is an extraordinary amount of lateral violence in the community that they're desperately trying to address. I have gone there a number of times to deliver training and facilitate initiatives to help combat the lateral and domestic violence that occurs there, but because the community is not seen as being disadvantaged there is little in the way of social services available. It is smaller organisations and community groups that are working to try to redress the issues within the community.

During one training session with a small group of workers I was advising them about strategies for their personal safety, and as I was delivering the training outside an Aboriginal man started chasing his wife and child down the street and attempting to spear his wife. Stunned, as I was delivering training about personal safety, I had to advise that for our own safety we could not directly intervene in the situation. Our own lives could have been in danger.

'How can you just ignore a child and woman in such danger?' was the question asked.

That was the dilemma: personal safety has to be taught, but what do you do when faced with a situation like that? It is an impossible choice, and one that is created because there had been a failure to address the underlying problems in that community that had caused the violence in the first place.

I believe just throwing money and resources at a problem doesn't solve it. There has to be thoughtful consideration about how those resources are deployed and an understanding of the community dynamics into which the funding is being placed. There is no one size fits all approach, and too often we think a particular policy or intervention will be some kind of magic pill that will solve all the issues for Aboriginal Australia.

What we need is to recognise the historical, intergenerational trauma that has been felt by Aboriginal communities during our colonial history. It has been internalised and now manifests as these kinds of extreme violent reactions against the perpetrator's own family and community members. The instances of lateral violence within communities are problems that need to be addressed, leading as it does not just to unsafe communities but high Aboriginal incarnation rates and unsafe domestic situations for Aboriginal women and children.

Too often these problems have been seen as nothing more than simple crimes, and no efforts have been made to relieve the source of the violence and unrest. We cannot just treat the violence through a punitive response, although anyone who commits violence against another must be censured. What we need to do is develop ways for the communities to process and deal with the underlying trauma and aggression that facilitates the violence.

Drugs and alcohol are convenient scapegoats for the causes of violence in remote and regional Aboriginal communities, yet while working in these areas I have seen the same levels of violent behaviour in dry communities where drugs and alcohol are effectively managed. We need to rethink how we are first framing and then approaching these issues, acknowledging the role of intergenerational trauma if we are to see any meaningful change for Aboriginal people.

38. SHARING MESSAGES

It's a lack of clarity that creates chaos and frustration. Those emotions are poison to any living goal.

– STEVE MARABOLI

I do think that what I do makes some difference, but I am just one person and my business, while growing with a number of effectively trained facilitators and assessors, has not been welcomed into every branch of child protection or every district. Even as I work within these agencies to advise and restructure the underlying issues about the ways in which we deal with child protection and social welfare within this country, I have seen up close how devastating getting it wrong can be.

In 2021, a few years after I set up my facilitator and training business, the children of one of my cousins was removed from her care reportedly because they were 'living in unclean conditions'. This meant that although there may have been concerns about the children there was absolutely no indication that the kids were in any sort of imminent danger or that, with effective help and guidance, the situation couldn't be rectified through supervisory contact and resources allocated to my cousin to help her maintain a home that the authorities deemed to be more suitable.

Instead of working with the family, the order was given for child protection officers to raid my cousin's house at 5.30 am, accompanied by police, and take the terrified children immediately from their beds. They were then taken to a hospital 50 kilometres away and placed under a child protection order that put all five children, aged from four months to seven years, into immediate care.

I was contracting to child protection services at the time, although in another district, so I was able to get onto a conference call with the child protection workers to request that the children be placed with their great grandparents, who had cared for the children in the past and whom the children knew very well. This was agreed to, and arrangements started to be organised. However, the case was taken over by a different office and the arrangements halted, and the children were to be placed separately in a variety of homes with carers who were not Aboriginal foster carers. I reminded the new manager of our child protection legislation, which stated that Aboriginal children should be placed first with family, second with Aboriginal carers and as a last resort with non-Aboriginal carers.

Legislation exists that gives families the right to request a family meeting to develop a family plan. It is known as family group conferencing (FGC) and I would easily be considered an expert on this topic, so naturally I requested an FGC and that a resolution be sought for the situation. My requests were summarily denied and the children remained separated in different foster care placements, their schools were changed and their worlds were turned upside down for the next eight to 12 months.

The response by the child protection agency was not only mishandled, but was unnecessary and over-reactive. Five children were removed because of concerns about neglect as a result of a dirty home, which was cleaned up the next day. In the following weeks it became clear that the entire exercise had been initiated by the white paternal grandmother of the youngest child, who wanted that child placed in her care and didn't have any regard for the welfare of any of the other children.

I could see how easily non-Aboriginal people and those with a hidden agenda could victimise perfectly respectable Aboriginal families using well-meaning but poorly exercised child protection mechanisms. In all cases, getting child protection involved in any matter should be a last resort and not be open to the manipulations of grandparents, non-custodial parents or members of the wider community who may have an axe to grind or feel dislike towards Aboriginal people. Time and time again I see what is supposed to be a positive service used and manipulated in ways that justify the suspicion held against it by Aboriginal communities.

Most children in the care system are in need of protection, but I have also come across some families that are guilty of nothing other than being Aboriginal and not conforming to the system. For those, a family meeting is absolutely vital in order to be heard and have the case settled in a way that is fair and reasonable.

As Aboriginal people, shouting from the outskirts and railing against the system, even when it is unfair, will likely label you as a troublemaker and make the caseworkers dig their heels in even deeper. However, if you choose to be quiet and compliant then decisions will be made whether you like them or not, and again your voice will not be heard. It is an impossible situation for Aboriginal people and means that no matter the veracity of the claims made against them, poor decisions continue to be made. Children can easily be used as pawns by those who have no interest in their actual welfare.

Working in this sector can make for a challenging and disillusioning life. I see so much success in engaging family to make their own decision, but I still witness some absolutely heartbreaking failures. I stay to fight, though, because someone has to. Without resistance even the small victories would never happen.

Even as I engaged with the welfare agencies to support families I kept returning to the thought that there had to be a better way than this. This imperfect system is not the only system we have. There is a universe of spirit energy and connection that can guide us all. Grass-roots activism, connections, conversations and storytelling are more powerful in conflict resolution than any of the so-called initiatives I have seen presented by government after government and welfare body after welfare body. If only we all had a way to connect with the spirits of the ancestors and the universe and truly commune with them, perhaps we could find a way through this.

At a leadership conference I had attended in 2009 I had listened to the same old people droning on about the same old ideas. Suddenly I had one of my 'A-ha' moments, a message from spirit that was powerful and irresistible.

I had been using tarot cards for years to help me connect with spirit and find ways to understand and interpret the messages and symbols I was being sent. Perhaps there was a way the cards could help with the situation. I knew instinctively that tarot cards were not the right tools, as they had a long and difficult history and connection with witchcraft and the occult that, although undeserved, was too powerful to overcome, but what if I came up with a new version of tarot cards? One that connected with this land, with Aboriginal people and with our spirit, our Dreaming, and offered ways for all of us, Aboriginal and non-Aboriginal, to commune with the ancestors and the spirit of our land.

I had no idea how to start the process of creating the cards, but I had for years been creating artworks that had been inspired by history and spirit. These artworks had been part of my healing, part of my storytelling and making sense of my life. There is a long tradition of art in all cultures taking us into the world of the sacred, past the literal and into the spiritual and symbolic.

I came home excited and began work, choosing and creating works that would form the basis of my card deck. As I worked I heard the ancestors speaking through me, telling me what symbols, colours and images to use. I felt the entire process had been channelled from the universe and that the ancestors spoke through me and into these cards, waiting to speak to whomever accessed their messages through them.

As I worked I never thought about how I would get these cards out into the world. I just knew I had to co-create them with the ancestral spirits, and soon I had a pack of beautiful cards designed and printed. I knew nothing about the publishing world so I self-published the cards, going back to my experience as a salesperson at market stalls and at Magickal Realm of selling directly to people. My cards were resonating, and I felt the shift in myself as more and more people spoke to me of the profound feelings of connection the cards afforded them. However, my reach was small. I desperately needed a larger distributor to get the cards out into the mainstream.

I created and expanded on a deck of Aboriginal spirit oracles that seamlessly integrated the many ancient belief systems of the world with Aboriginal spirituality and wisdom. It forged the tools I had first begun to think about in the church at my friend's funeral and had gained even more from on the grounds of Glastonbury Abbey, where I had reconnected with the old ancient European ideal of the goddess. Here was a way I could communicate that essential truth, that all belief systems were one and that all spirituality came from the one great spirit. As I worked on the artwork for the cards I felt the universe smiling down on me, letting me know that I had finally come to the true pathway of my Dreaming. It helped me draw all the threads of my life, thoughts and beliefs together.

After a while I started to find people who shared my vision for the cards, and they were picked up by a visionary publisher I still work with today who was instrumental in getting them out into the world and encouraging me to continue the story through writing the book you are now reading.

I am proud that the cards exist and have been translated for other countries of the world, and that I have managed to share these messages as a way of starting to change the ways in which we talk about ourselves, our spirit, our Aboriginality, our difference and our similarities. I don't own the oracles, for ownership is a concept of colonialism and conflict; I own them no more than I own my children. I simply helped to create them and sent them out into the world. They are as the ancestors wanted them to be, and it was they who got together to help me communicate their messages to the world.

I think that if the ancestors ever suspected I was taking advantage or not honouring them and their gift they would remove my ability to do the work and share their message. One of the things Aboriginal spirituality can offer the world is the ability to let go of the need to possess, and to instead find ways to accommodate and listen to all and share all with generosity and kindness.

I believe that is why I have been incarnated into this life, into this body, to experience the world as an Aboriginal woman finding her identity so I could share that experience with everyone. When I move on from this life into the next and the next I know I will bring the wisdom of my experiences and resist the temptation to live one small, selfish life. If we all believed that we could change the world for the better, for it is not governments, authorities or systems that change things. It is people, and the stories we tell and actions we take.

We are more than our challenges, experiences, setbacks and triumphs. We are all part of the fabric of the universe, and if we can work to understand it then we can move past the concerns, pettiness and injustice and into the limitless generosity of spirit.

EPILOGUE

One of the hardest things I found in writing this book was how to end it. It felt so final, like a eulogy, and for a long time I grappled with what an ending could look like. As I was speaking with my girlfriend one day she wisely said to me, 'This isn't the end, Mel, this is just this part of your story. It's part of your family's story, and it doesn't end just because your book has.'

Her words were so wise and made so much sense that I finally understood how to finish the book, because this isn't the end. I've still got so much more life to live, so many more stories to make, and each day I'm still making them. It's my history and I'm still creating it. There will always be more to tell, about me, my family and my life. Who knows: I may even be blessed enough to add some grandchildren stories to my collection.

Where does it end? Maybe it doesn't. Maybe it just continues, like life does, even into the voices of the new generations and the new incarnations our souls may inhabit in the future and the past. I started my story looking out on a castle on a hill, a moment in time peeking through the sliver of curtains at remnants of the past. I've realised this is what life is all about: that brief moment, the sliver we experience that becomes our history.

Now I come to the end of this story . . . well, not the end of my story, because stories like mine don't really have endings. They play out through lifetimes and across eons and have many disappointments, losses and sadness, but also moments of triumphant celebration and love. So much love. Yes, there is also trauma. The tears from my past are long gone, but the memories of those days form part of who I am and are why I'm able to connect with and heal and assist others. I hope hearing my story will help you connect with your own stories, your own lifetimes then and now.

While we are experiencing a particular moment in our lives it can feel like it's taking forever, but it's literally just a moment in time, one moment of one life. There were times when I thought the pain, tears and trauma would never end, but somehow I was able to emerge from the depths of despair and each time take my life back. It won't happen like that for everyone, but for those who simply live to tell their story and can even manage to laugh about it, I applaud you!

I think that's the moral of my story: we can all have trauma in our lives, and our trauma can destroy us or define us. I guess from the very beginning of my conception I'd always been a fighter, starting with my fight to live and be born. We can choose to be a victim or we can stand up and take back the power that has been taken from us.

I want to finish up the same way in which I started my book. Once more I'm sitting out looking into the distance, this time in the castle that is Michael's and my house on the far north coast of New South Wales, Australia. I'm looking across my pool over to the valley in the distance where banana plantations grow. I can hear the cows mooing below at the bottom of the creek, and if I listen hard enough and the breeze blows the right way I can hear the traffic way down on the highway passing by, the drivers never knowing that someone is noticing their passing. I often wonder about that, the people passing. How are they today? What's happening for them? What are they listening to? Is someone waiting for them on the other end of their journey? I hope so. As it turns out there were people waiting for me, and I am so grateful for them: my beautiful husband Michael, my children, grandchildren and greater family who are here to help me enjoy this part of what is, really, an unfinished journey after all.

I leave you now as I continue travelling down my highway and hope for you, as for me, there will always be someone waiting for you to get home.

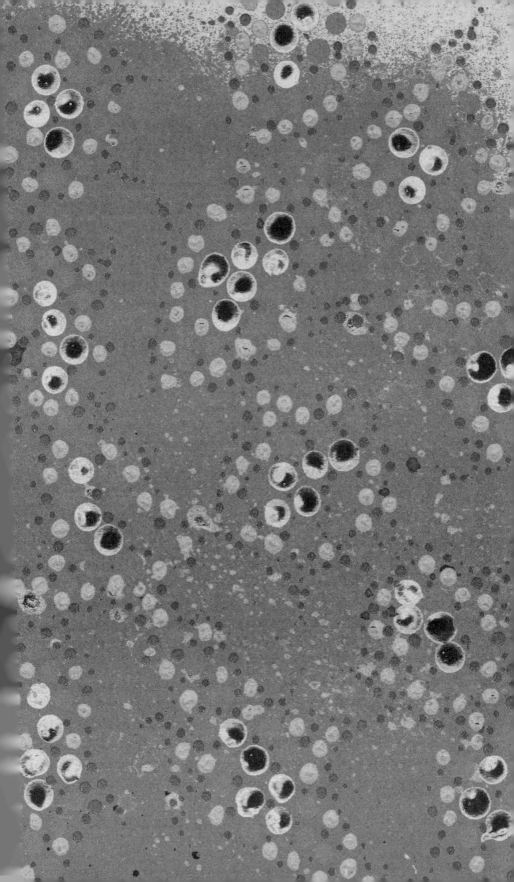

SERVICES AVAILABLE FOR HELP

If you have been affected by any of the information or themes in this book and need to contact a counselling, referral or support service, the contacts below may be helpful.

Please note these services are current as of 2024 and contact details are subject to change over time.

1800Respect

1800 737 732 ◆ www.1800respect.org.au

1800Respect is a free, confidential service that provides information, counselling and support for anyone experiencing domestic or family violence. The website includes a comprehensive database of services for housing, counselling, welfare and financial support, legal services, health care, surviving workplace harassment and domestic and/or sexual violence available across all Australian states and territories.

13YARN

13 92 76 ◆ www.13yarn.org.au

This national crisis support line is for Aboriginal and Torres Strait Islander people who are feeling overwhelmed or are having difficulty coping.

Beyond Blue

1300 22 4636 ◆ https://www.beyondblue.org.au

This mental health information and referral line is available to individuals across Australia.

Blue Knot

1300 657 380 ◆ blueknot.org.au

The Blue Knot helpline and redress support service provides information and support for anyone across Australia affected by complex trauma, including repeated, ongoing or extreme interpersonal trauma, violence, abuse, neglect or exploitation experienced as a child, young person and/or adult.

Lifeline

13 11 14 ◆ www.lifeline.org.au

Lifeline is a 24/7 telephone counselling service available Australia wide. If you are experiencing crisis or depression or just feeling overwhelmed and need to speak with someone who will listen, Lifeline can provide support via telephone, text or online chat. Lifeline in the community also offers face-to-face counselling, bereavement support groups and financial counselling, as well as suicide and domestic and family violence response training

Men's Helpline Australia

1300 789 978 ◆ https://mensline.org.au/

This confidential telephone counselling service is for men anywhere, any time.

No to Men's Violence

Referral service: 1300 766 491 ◆ ntv.org.au

This peak advocacy, training, referral and counselling service is focused on preventing male violence against women and children through encouraging men to acknowledge and take accountability for their violent behaviour.

Your Toolkit

yourtoolkit.org.au

This online information service is designed to provide assistance to women experiencing family or domestic violence. The site offers practical steps to assist women to safely escape dangerous relationships and situations.

SUPPORT SERVICES FOR VICTIMS

Victim support services vary by state, with many operating through the crime and justice or police services. They can offer help with reporting a crime as well as providing referrals for counselling, financial assistance for immediate needs and economic loss and recognition payment, as well as referrals and information about state-specific domestic violence, welfare and mental health services.

Australian Capital Territory
Victim Support ACT (VSACT) Human Rights Commission
1800 822 272
ACT Human Rights Commission,
56 Allara Street, Canberra City 2600

New South Wales
Victims Services 1800 633 063
Aboriginal Contact Line 1800 019 123
www.victimsservices.justice.nsw.gov.au

Northern Territory
Victims of Crime NT (VOCNT)
1800 672 242 (seven-day/24-hour phone line)
victimsofcrime.org.au

Queensland
Victim Assist
1300 546 587 (business hours)
www.qld.gov.au/law/crime-and-police/victims-and-witnesses-of-crime/request-victim-of-crime-information

South Australia
Victim Support Service (VSS)
1800 842 846
www.victimsa.org

Tasmania
Victim Support Service
www.justice.tas.gov.au/victims/services/victims-of-crime-service
1300 663 773 or (03) 6165 7524
Level 1, 54 Victoria Street, Hobart 7000

Victoria
Victims of Crime Helpline
1800 819 817 (8 am – 11 pm)
https://www.victimsofcrime.vic.gov.au/

Western Australia
Victim Support Service
1800 818 988
Level 2, District Court Building
500 Hay Street, Perth 6000

ABORIGINAL LEGAL AND SUPPORT SERVICES

Aboriginal Family Legal Service Western Australia
(08) 9355 1502 ♦ www.afls.org.au
113 Orrong Road, Rivervale 6103

Aboriginal Family Legal Services Queensland
Offices in Toowoomba, Murgon and Gympie
www.aflsq.org.au

*Aboriginal Legal Service New South Wales
and Australian Capital Territory*
1800 765 767 ♦ www.alsnswact.org.au

Djirra (Victoria)
1800 105 303 ♦ djirra.org.au
This organisation provides legal and support services for Aboriginal
people and non-Aboriginal people with Aboriginal children who are
experiencing family and domestic violence.

Northern Territory government Aboriginal legal referral service
nt.gov.au/law/processes/get-legal-advice/indigenous-legal-services

ACKNOWLEDGEMENTS

To my beautiful husband, a constant source of support during times when I was reliving the chaos of my past. His unwavering reminders of the life we share today kept me moving forward.

My incredible children Jessica, Daniel, Teniel, Cassie and Jenna, for their understanding as I learned to be a parent alongside them and their forgiveness for the many mistakes I made along the way.

To my precious grandbabies, each of you bring me so much joy. You are my love and my light.

To my family, Mum, Dad and Shannon, for allowing me to share our story, embracing the good, the bad and the ugly. We each survived this life in our unique ways.

Gratitude extends to the many people woven into my narrative. Without their presence, my story might have been different.

To Lisa, Paul, Katie, Sara, Gabiann and the Rockpool team, your belief in me, the gift of time and space during moments when I couldn't continue and the recognition of my story's value are treasures beyond measure.

Lastly, a humble acknowledgement to the universe and my ancestors. You've granted me the life I live today, instilling the courage to find my way through darkness and the gratitude to revel in the light.

ABOUT THE AUTHOR

Mel Brown is an Indigenous author, artist and clairvoyant who has written and illustrated many popular spiritual titles.

She has a Masters in Indigenous Healing and Trauma from Southern Cross University in Lismore, New South Wales, Australia and many years of experience working with children at risk. Acclaimed for her expertise in cultural competency and lateral violence both nationally and internationally, Mel draws on both her personal and professional experience to work with families and organisations to ensure Aboriginal children who are unable to live at home are not excluded from cultural connection with their families.

spiritdreaming.com.au